DUNMORE POTTERY

A contemporary account

with additional commentary by

GRAEME CRUICKSHANK

MA, AMA, FMA, FSA Scot

SCOTTISH POTTERY STUDIES No. 4

THE
STIRLING
SMITH

2002

Previous titles in the series:

No. 1 Scottish Spongeware (1982): out of print

No. 2 Scottish Saltglaze (1982)

No. 3 Campsie Ware (1992)

By the same author:

Scottish Pottery: a brief history (Shire Publications, 1987)

738·37

SCOTTISH POTTERY STUDIES
No. 4 A Visit to Dunmore Pottery
ISBN 0-9525-332-78
© Graeme D. R. Cruickshank
Stirling, 2002

Foreword

SCOTTISH POTTERY STUDIES is the name of a series of booklets, the aim of each being to examine some specific aspect of Scottish Pottery history. The scheme was initiated in 1980 as the result of a bequest from Frank E. Cruickshank of Aberdeen, and the first booklets in what was intended to be a regular series appeared in 1982. This author researched, compiled, scripted, designed, produced, and distributed the booklets, but the high cost of printing and involved mechanics of marketing has meant that the series has not progressed with the regularity originally anticipated. I am therefore very grateful that the next two booklets have been published by public bodies, thereby relieving me of some of the practical chores: Glasgow City Libraries in 1992, and the Stirling Smith Art Gallery & Museum on this occasion. I would particularly like to thank the Director of the latter institution, Elspeth King, for her assistance and encouragement with this latest booklet.

G.D.R.C.
Edinburgh, July 2002

Dedication

I would like to dedicate this booklet to the memory of Professor James Spreull (1908-1998), it being the first substantial publication which I have brought out since his death. He was a notable collector of Scottish pottery at a time when it was not as highly regarded as nowadays, and did much to kindle my enthusiasm for the subject by his expressions of knowledge, intuition, and wit. At lectures and seminars about various aspects of Scottish Pottery, it was his wont gently to introduce a note of controversy, sit back and wait until those of differing opinions were ranged against each other ready to do battle, and then exclaim with a mischievous chuckle: "The pot still boils!"

Acknowledgements

Quite a number of people have been helpful in various ways during the preparation of this booklet, among whom I would like to mention the following (in alphabetical order):

Susan Anderson (Philadelphia Museum of Art), Stuart and Pauline Baird, Beverley Casebow (Huntly House Museum), Pamela Clark (Royal Archives), John Dickson (Falkirk Council Community Services), Anne Countess of Dunmore, Geoffrey Godden, Stanley K. Hunter (Scottish Exhibitions Study Group), Willie Johnston (Royal Highland and Agricultural Society of Scotland Library), Elma Lindsay (Stirling Libraries, Heritage and Culture Service), John Mackay (General Register Office for Scotland), Robert Rankine, Neal Spencer (British Museum), Brian Watters, and all those who have allowed items of pottery to be photographed and reproduced here. In terms of production, I wish to thank Heather Jack for the specially-undertaken photography, Nicola Bodman and Duncan Gray for the location maps, Hilary O'Donnell for typing a manuscript imbued with powers of seemingly infinite expansion which would have tested the explanatory prowess of Stephen Hawking, Michael McGinnes for working wonders with his computer-scanning of all the illustrative material, and Trevor Andrews and his team at Art-is-an Option in Alloa for putting it all together.

Finally, I must say thank you to Elizabeth Ramsay for lending me an original printing of the booklet *A Visit to Dunmore Pottery* in 1975 (I have not encountered one since), and for allowing me to reproduce it with a view to future republication. Sadly, shortly after I returned the booklet to her, she was killed in a car crash. All I know of the person who actually owned the said booklet is that they were a friend of Mrs Ramsay, and having been unable to discover any further information as to their identity, I am unable to thank them for permitting the booklet to be reprinted, or even to secure their permission. If they happen to read this present booklet, I hope that they will approve of what has been done.

CONTENTS

Frontispiece

List of illustrations

Front cover. Dish in the form of a leaf, glazed in 'autumn colours'. Width 8½ ins. The central area of the back of this leaf dish, which contains the potter's mark, is reproduced on the back cover of this booklet. (Photograph by Heather Jack.)

Frontispiece. Catherine, 6th Countess of Dunmore, "that truly excellent lady", who was Peter Gardner's most enthusiastic supporter. (Reproduced from an etching by J. Jenkins II of a painting by Robert Thorburn, published in *Portraits of the Female Artistocracy of the Court of Queen Victoria* compiled by William and Edward Finden (London, 1849), vol. I, unpaginated.) Here vignetted.

Figure 1.   Location map showing Dunmore Pottery in relation to towns and villages in the region.

Figure 2.   Location map showing Dunmore Pottery in relation to features in the district. (Both maps generated by Nicola Bodman and Duncan Gray.)

Figure 3.   Frontispiece to the booklet *A Visit to Dunmore Pottery*, actual size.

Figure 4.   Signboard for Potterland Farm in Kirkcudbrightshire; the farm buildings may be seen in the distance, nestling at the foot of Potterland Hill. (Photograph by Graeme Cruickshank.)
Reproduced by kind permission of Historic Scotland © Crown Copyright

Figure 5.   Badge of the Highland and Agricultural Society of Scotland (designed by John Clerk of Eldin), the organisation which gave Peter Gardner the opportunity to reach a wide audience. (Reproduced from the title page of the annual Show catalogues.)

Figure 6.   Advertisement by Alexander Jenkinson, the retailer who gave Peter Gardner the opportunity to reach a wide audience. (Reproduced from *The Scotsman*, 28th July 1874.)

Figure 7.   The Duke and Duchess of Edinburgh in *ca.* 1874, the first members of the Royal Family to patronise Peter Gardner. (Contemporary photograph by F. Backofen.)
Reproduced by kind permission of the Royal Archives © 2002 Her Majesty Queen Elizabeth II

Figure 8.   Advertisement by Peter Gardner for his display of Dunmore ware at the Highland Show. (Reproduced from *The Scotsman*, 26th July 1880.)

Figure 9.   Advertisement for Dunmore Art Pottery. (Reproduced from the *Pottery Gazette Diary*, 1885, p.163.) (My thanks to Geoffrey Godden for informing me of this important item.)

Figure 10.   The Gardner family tombstone in Airth Kirkyard.
Figure 11.   The inscription on the above. (Both photographs by Graeme Cruickshank.)

Figure 12.   Advertisement for Dunmore Pottery. (Reproduced from the *Falkirk Herald*, 18th March 1905.)

Figure 52.   Larbert Station, in the 1890s, from a contemporary postcard produced by Mrs Cockburn, newsagent in Larbert. It shows the new station, widened and with greatly extended platforms. The steam locomotive is a Drummond rebuild of a Conner 2-4-0 No. 30.
Reproduced by kind permission of Tom McGhie, Archivist of the Caledonian Railway Association
A photograph (present location not known) of the previous Larbert Station, a charming building which was replaced by the one shown here in 1892, appears on the front cover of *Old Larbert and Stenhousemuir* by Guthrie Hutton (Ochiltree, 1995). There is a later photograph in the same book showing the covered bridge at Larbert Station and a length of platform, but no buildings, although there is an engine in full steam (*op.cit.*, p.21).

Figure 53.   Airth Station, in 1960, six years after it closed. It was subsequently demolished. (Photograph by W.A.C. Smith.)

Figure 54.   Close-up of the sheet music held by the singing frog; cf. Figue C1.
Reproduced by kind permission of Falkirk Museums

Figure 55.   Hand-powered potter's wheel. (Drawing reproduced from *Scottish Pottery* by Arnold Fleming (Glasgow, 1923), Plate V, opp. p.52.)

Figure 56.   Potting in Ancient Egypt, as depicted on a painted relief frieze in the Mastaba of Ti at Saqqara. (Drawing reproduced from *Le Tombeau de Ti* by Lucienne Épron *et al.* (Cairo, 1913), Plate 71.)

Figure 57.   Part of the main kiln at Dunmore Pottery in a state of partial collapse in 1974, showing the damaging effects of the penetrating roots of silver birch trees growing around the top of the cylindrical section. (Photograph by Graeme Cruickshank.)
Three details of the main kiln:

Figure 58.   Arched brickwork, looking past main doorway through inner doorway.
Figure 59.   do., exterior of south-west vent.
Figure 60.   do., interior of north-west vent.
(These three photographs by Ken Mackay.)
Figure 61.   Plan of Dunmore main kiln, at CC.
Figure 62.   Elevation, do.
Figure 63.   Section, do., at AA.
Figure 64.   Section, do., at BB.
(These reconstruction drawings by Ken Mackay.)

Figure 65.   Ordnance Survey 25-inch map of 1859/60, showing Dunmore Pottery.
Figure 66.   do., of 1895.
Figure 67.   do., of 1913.
These three maps reproduced by kind permission of the Trustees of the National Library of Scotland

Colour Section

Fancy Frogs

The five single pots illustrated in the 'Visit' booklet

Figure C7.   Pot similar to Queen's Vase (named).   Width 12 ins.   (Photograph by Heather Jack.)

Figure C8.   Dunmore Toad (named). Length 6½ ins. (though some examples are much bigger). (Photograph by Heather Jack.)

Three types of ware mentioned in the 'Visit' booklet

Figure C9.   Vase with cracquelure glaze effect, pale green on dark green. Height 3 ins.
Reproduced by kind permission of Glasgow Museums

Figure C10. Close-up of cracquelure glaze effect, orange on pea-green. (In enlarged form, this is featured on the cover, both front and back, of the booklet produced by Falkirk Museums in 2002, compiled by Geoff Bailey, on local ceramics in the Falkirk District, including Dunmore ware. The item itself is in the collections at Callendar House, Falkirk.)
Reproduced by kind permission of Falkirk Museums

Figure C11. Vase of agate ware, giving the striped effect, with additional spatter glaze. Height 4 ins.
Reproduced by kind permission of Glasgow Museums

Figure C12. Teapot with silver mountings, hallmarked Glasgow, 1882/3, R. & G. D. (R. & G. Drummond, 128 Buchanan Street). Diameter 4½ ins.
Reproduced by kind permission of Glasgow Museums

Eight notable items of Dunmore ware

Figure C13.   Loop-handled bowl with rustic body; rim and handle of simulated wicker-work. A good example of a Dunmore pseudomorph. Height 5½ ins.

Figure C14. Cluster of four vases, thrown separately but fixed and glazed as a single unit. Height 4½ ins.

Figure C15. Jug in the form of a satyr head. Height 4½ ins.

Figure C16. Pickle dish in the form of a gherkin on a leaf. Length 5½ ins.

Figure C17. Bowl with double loop-handles. Height 4½ ins.

Figure C18. Jug with long and narrow neck, flaring towards the rim. Height 4½ ins.

Figure C19. Wall vase in the form of the leaf-nest of a weaver bird, which perches above it. Height 10 ins.

Figure C20. Cluster of four vases, one carrying elegant decoration sitting on top of a tree trunk to which three more are tied with twine. Three lesser hollow trunks act as additional flower-holders (making seven in all), alternating with a repeated little figure of a weary maiden who is sitting down, resting her load. Height 14 ins.
This group of eight reproduced by kind permission of Glasgow Museums

Some other special Dunmore items

Figure C21. Loop-handled bowl exhibiting four different methods in its making – throwing, extruding, moulding, and cutting. Height 5½ ins. (Photograph by Heather Jack.)

Figure C22. Jug in the form of a dragon, with bright scarlet glaze (the red dragon of Wales?). Height 14 ins. (Photograph by Robin Hill.)

Figure C23. Wall vase in the form of a crayfish, with thick turquoise glaze. Height 9½ ins.
Reproduced by kind permission of Glasgow Museums

Figure C24. Bowl with multi-coloured spattered glazes. Diameter 3 ins. (Photograph by Heather Jack.)

From the Dunmore Pottery House lavatory

Figure C25. Wall-mounted urinal, with dabbed glaze. Height 11½ ins.

Figure C26. Floor tile with decorative device. Height 5½ ins.

Figure C27. Another similar tile. Height 5 ins.
These three objects are reproduced by kind permission of the Royal Commission on the Ancient and Historical Monuments of Scotland © Crown Copyright

Figure C28. Chinese-style bowl, the form of which imitates, or perhaps even copies, a bronze prototype. Diameter 7½ ins. (Photograph by Heather Jack.)

Figure C29. Airth Kirkyard, showing the author holding his prize piece of Dunmore ware beside the grave of Peter Gardner. (Photograph by Robert Rankine.)

The tiled room in Dunmore Pottery House

Figure C30. Tiled section of wall, showing (a) cornice in turquoise; (b) row of relief moulded tiles; (c) two rows of highly-colourful spatter-glazed tiles; (d) row of brown (quasi-mahogany?) tiles. Square tiles 6 x 6 ins.

Figure C31. Part of door with tiled panels, showing classical heads, men in turquoise and women in ochre, plus finger-plates; also part of the above tiled wall.

Figure C32. Part of the tiled fire surround: upper, a Bacchanalian scene in turquoise; lower, a tile displaying the royal coat of arms, flanked by more relief moulded tiles. (Photographs by Ken Mackay.)

The Dunmore kiln

Figure C33. The main kiln at Dunmore Pottery, shortly before its collapse in 1974. (Photograph by Willie More.)

Preface

The making of pottery is one of the most ancient crafts known to man, and in Scotland this dates back not just for centuries but for millenia. The great era of Scottish pottery production, however, was from the middle of the 18th century to the early decades of the 20th century. After that, the loss of markets caused by the Great War, and the Depression of the 1920s, brought about the almost total extinction of the Scottish pottery industry. Most of the great factories failed, closed down, and were swept away, unlamented and unrecorded. Now that there is so much interest in the Scottish potteries and their products, the problem of lack of information is becoming ever more apparent, and tracing the history of any particular pottery has to rely for the most part on mere scraps of information, and the end product must of necessity be fragmentary and incomplete. Nevertheless, there is a great deal of information to be found, even though much of it lurks in somewhat obscure places. First-hand accounts of Scottish potteries in operation are not common, and therefore when one is discovered it is a matter of considerable interest. This interest is heightened when the subject happens to be one of the most intriguing of the Scottish potworks, the Dunmore Pottery near Airth in Stirlingshire. Its wares, which were often novel both in shape and in decoration, were highly popular in its own day, and are avidly collected now. Indeed, they may be rated as second only to the much-vaunted Wemyss Ware of Kirkcaldy as being sought after by modern enthusiasts of old Scottish pottery. It is therefore curious that there is no detailed account of the history of Dunmore Pottery, and the few short articles and notes in various sources fall far short of providing a comprehensive portrayal of the firm's activities.[1]

A definitive history of Dunmore Pottery is sorely needed, but this present booklet is not it, nor has it any pretensions to be. In essence, it takes a look at one episode in the life of the Pottery, when it was visited by a reporter of some perception, the account being published in the form of a small booklet. The text and illustrations are reprinted here, some additional commentary is offered, and a few themes are expanded. Extensive use has been made of illustrative material, and as an alternative to captions, each illustration will carry only a Figure number, the description and relevance of the illustration being explained in the text, where it will be cross-referenced. For ease of identification of any particular illustration, refer to the list near the front of the booklet. Colour illustrations have a separate sequence of Figure numbers, prefixed by the letter C. Much of the work for this booklet was done in the mid 1980s, and written up during a sojourn in the highlands of Papua New Guinea in 1987. It has lain unfinished since that time, but 2002, being the centenary of Peter Gardner's death, seemed an appropriate moment to revive the subject, chase down a few more sidelines, and see it through to publication. Indeed, it is the occasion of that centenary which has spurred me on, and in particular has resulted in the note on Peter Gardner being much longer and more detailed than was originally intended. My one frustration has been that in order to bring out this booklet to coincide with the Gardner centenary exhibition in Stirling Museum, not every avenue of investigation has been followed with the degree of thoroughness I would have liked. Perhaps this work will inspire a more thorough-going account of Dunmore Pottery and its remarkable products to be undertaken.

Introduction

Dunmore Pottery was situated in the former county of Stirlingshire, on the south side of the River Forth, approximately halfway between the towns of Stirling and Falkirk in east-central Scotland (see Figure 1). It lay hard by Dunmore Moss to the east, being about 1½ miles south-

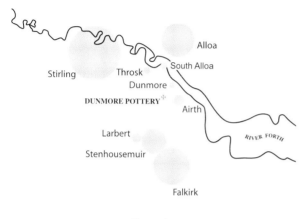

Figure 1

west of the little village of Dunmore, and slightly further to the west of the small town of Airth (see Figure 2). It should come as no surprise that a venture such as pottery making was established in the vicinity of Dunmore, for the two basic essentials were available in abundance: clay and coal. This is made clear in the *Statistical Account of Scotland*, in which Rev. Robert Ure wrote of the parish of Airth thus: "The soil is, in general, a strong deep clay…there is a fine coal under the rock in both hills [Airth and Dunmore], and in the flat fields around".[2] The geological composition of the district may stem from one of nature's most dramatic and destructive forces – a gigantic wave. The evidence takes the form of ancient whale bones, which have been discovered at more than a dozen sites in the Carse of Stirling. The presence of these animals so far inland, together with deposits of a type of sand normally found on the coast of Norway, points to a *tsunami* (huge wave) washing over this area of east-central Scotland around 10,000 years ago.[3] There are several reasons which may explain the siting of the original Dunmore Pottery beside Dunmore Moss when considered in relation to an account of the countryside around it written by Richard Gillespie in 1880. Firstly, "The moss lies upon carse-clay",[4] thereby allowing the raw material of pottery making to be obtained without undue labour. Secondly, "across the dark expanse are numerous piles of peat which

have been cast and stacked by the local farmers for boiler fires, and sale in the outlying villages, and of the fuels obtained from the earth's crust, the most obvious and accessible is peat", which was used to fire kilns in some rural areas of Scotland in pre-industrial times. Also, some glaze constituents, such as copper, may have been obtained from the Ochil Hills north of Alloa. Another potentially useful substance was a lot closer to hand,

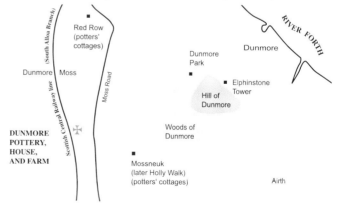

Figure 2

considering that Dunmore Moss sat immediately adjacent: "A moss litter company of considerable age sends moss to the pottery-manufacturing areas of England where it is used for packing china".[5] That being the case in 1953, it would be surprising if Dunmore Pottery had not utilised this moss for packing its own wares.

The earliest printed reference to the production of pottery in Scotland so far discovered refers to Throsk, just a couple of miles away from Dunmore, of which Sir Robert Sibbald wrote in 1710: "Here is a Potterie, where Earthen Pots, and severall other Leam Vessels are made".[6] ('Leam', more commonly 'lame', is an old term meaning china or earthenware.) This was indeed a long-running concern; waster finds indicate that it was under way in the post-medieval period, and it continued right through the era of Dunmore's fame, closing about the same time. From the description of the products of Throsk Pottery given by Arnold Fleming in *Scottish Pottery*, it would seem to have been turning out the same type of goods as Dunmore Pottery in the pre Peter Gardner days, but thereafter Throsk became better known as a brick and tile works.[7] It therefore did not pose any threat of rivalry as Peter Gardner developed his new range of products at Dunmore. Throsk was not alone in being an early site for pottery production in the area. Even closer to Dunmore was Poppletrees, and there is a passing reference in the accounts of Spittal's Hospital in Stirling, dated 1626, to the piggers of Poppletrees ('pig' is an old Scottish word for a pot; hence 'piggers' were potters). Indeed, this whole area seems to have supported a thriving pottery trade in the pre-industrial era.[8] It is also worth noting that the Stirling burgh records have given us the earliest-known name of a potter in Scotland, when they recorded a pigmaker named Moffat in 1521.

Pottery production at Dunmore itself was under way not long after that earliest known reference to Throsk. It features in MacFarlane's *Geographical Collections*, in a section dealing with several parishes in the Falkirk/Stirling area, including Airth, which was compiled in 1723 by Alexander Johnstoun of Kirkland. It does not actually refer to Dunmore by that name, but by its older appellation of Elphingstone (both the 'g' and the 'e' are optional): "A mile North Northwest from the house and Kirk of Airth stands the house of Elphingstone upon the south side of the Forth where is a harbour for ships…At Elphingstone are salt pans, coal pits, a fire engine to work the coal and potters, here is a fir park".[9] Despite the odd syntax of that last sentence, it is interesting to have a literary reference to pottery production in Scotland at such an early date, as these are not common for the pre-industrial period (*i.e.* pre 1750). Another appears later in the century, being contained in William Nimmo's *General History of Stirlingshire* of 1777: "Paper milns and bleachfields, of good reputation, are erected in sundry parts of the shire, as also tyle and brickworks, with potteries for earthen vessels, and these not only for home consumption, but also for foreign export".[10] It is a pity that subsequent editions of the work, published in 1817 and 1880 under different editors, did not enlarge upon this note, or even apparently retain it. More regrettable still is the situation regarding those twin pillars of Scottish local studies, the Old and New Statistical Accounts, when they come to deal with the parish of Airth. The *OSA* (1792) quite fails to mention pottery making, while the *NSA* (1841) actually excludes it: "Weaving is the only species of manufacture carried on, and that to a small extent".[11] It was left to the *Third Statistical Account* (1953) to make reference to what was long past: "Of the other dead industries perhaps the most well-known was the pottery of Peter Gardiner [the accustomed misspelling] at Dunmore. Mr Gardiner was noted for the red and green glazes he produced and for his leaf and vegetable designs".[12]   Other local histories tend to pay it scant regard; for instance, Archibald McMichael, while dealing with the parish of Airth around 1890, merely says: "Agriculture is the principal industry, but some of the inhabitants are employed in the manufacture of pottery and the quarrying of freestone".[13] For all the plaudits it had won from royalty, the nobility, and connoisseurs, and its popularity with ordinary people, Dunmore pottery did not always receive its due share of attention.

Before the turn of the 18th century, the Pottery had come into the hands of the Gardner family, with whom it was to become principally associated. (In the early days, they spelt their surname with an 'i'.) Peter Gardiner, who bore the same name as his father, was noted as being a potter in the parish of Airth in 1797. One son, William (born 1789), took over the running of Alloa Pottery after possibly gaining work experience in Glasgow, while a younger son, John (born 1797), who might have assisted both his father and elder brother at Dunmore, duly took over there and laid the foundations for the Pottery's future success. It was his son, Peter Gardner (born 1834), who was to achieve fame for Dunmore with his unorthodox shapes and spectacular glaze effects, though this did not happen immediately. His father died in 1866, but it was not until 1874, with the launch of the 'new Dunmore', that the Pottery was set on a course destined to achieve widespread acclaim. It was arguably Scotland's most successful foray into the milieu of art pottery, though by no means the only one – in addition to the famous Wemyss Ware of Kirkcaldy, there were other notable exponents such as the Seaton Pottery in Aberdeen; nor should factories be overlooked when they contained art sections, such as the Port Dundas Pottery in Glasgow, producing saltglazed and impasto wares, and Buchan's Pottery at Portobello, making the so-called 'Portobello Faience' (which was in reality closely akin to the Silicon ware of Doulton of Lambeth).

During the last quarter of the 19th century, Dunmore products earned a high reputation and Peter Gardner rose to a position of eminence in the world of art pottery. At the height of his prowess, the works were visited by a perceptive reporter, and it is his account, published in the form of a booklet in or about 1887, which forms the core of this study. It consisted of 10 pages, each measuring 4 inches by 6¾ inches, comprising a frontispiece, a proclamation, and eight pages of text and illustration. The final seven pages were numbered 4 to 10, and each was headed "A Visit to Dunmore Pottery" in Gothic script. The entire frontispiece [p.1] and proclamation [p.2], together with the main heading [on p.3], are reproduced in this booklet, prior to the reprint of the text.

By the end of the 19th century, Peter Gardner's health was failing, and his death in 1902 marked the end of the great phase of Dunmore production. It was not the end of the Pottery, though, and it survived for another dozen years at least. Its closing date is not known with certainty; it seems to have been still functioning at the outbreak of the First World War, but unlikely to have kept going until the end of it. The main kiln stood until 1974, a mute sentinel to the glory days of Peter Gardner, and it is his story that we should examine next.

Frontispiece to the Booklet

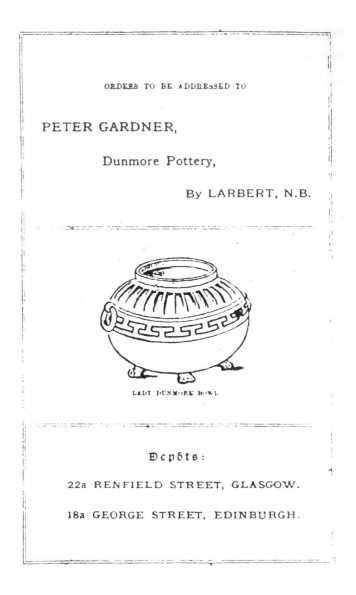

ORDERS TO BE ADDRESSED TO

PETER GARDNER,

Dunmore Pottery,

By LARBERT, N.B.

LADY DUNMORE BOWL

Depôts:

22a RENFIELD STREET, GLASGOW.

18a GEORGE STREET, EDINBURGH.

Figure 3

As this writer is unaware of the location of an original printing of the booklet under review, it is difficult to assess if this is the frontispiece, or the actual cover. It consists of three parts: (I) the name and address of the potter and his pottery, (II) an illustration of a highly significant piece of Dunmore ware, and (III) the addresses of two pottery depots in the big cities.

(I)

Orders to be addressed to
PETER GARDNER,
Dunmore Pottery,
By LARBERT, N.B.

Clearly, Peter Gardner was the top man at Dunmore Pottery, and so it is appropriate that he should become of first subject of study, and in particular, the manner in which he made his breakthrough into the world of art pottery. He was born at Dunmore Pottery in 1833, son of John Gardner and grandson of Peter Gardiner, both of whom had run the Pottery successively before him.[14] It should be said here that there has been some confusion about his date of birth. In the Census of 1841, his age is given as 7 years, indicating a birth-year of 1834, but the Census Returns are not consistent. He is absent from Airth parish in 1851 and 1861, but in 1871 he is given as aged 34, and in 1881 as 44, both yielding a birth-year of 1837. In 1891, however, he is down as being 56, giving a birth-year of 1835, and in 1901 as 64, giving a birth-year of 1837. Thus the five Censuses in which Peter Gardner appears give his birth-year variously as 1834, 1835, and 1837 (three times). To resolve this, recourse must be made to the Old Parish Registers, now held in the General Register Office in Edinburgh, though even this source contains an unsettling ambiguity. The record of Peter Gardner's birth is there all right, but there is some degree of dubiety as to the year. The entries occur in more or less chronological order, with the year as a general heading and only day and month given for each one individually. However, late insertions properly belonging to the previous year are not uncommon, and indeed they sometimes belong to two or three years beforehand, and in these instances the year *is* stated beside the individual entry. The entry relating to Peter Gardner appears right at the bottom of the page; the two preceding entries have the year-date 1833, but above them is a series (without single year-dates) under the general heading of 1834. Given the pattern of dating described above, the presumption must be that the Gardner entry belongs to 1834. The actual wording reads: "John Gardener [*sic*] and Helen Cathie had a child born 7th June and baptized 29th June called Peter".[15]

Considering his birth-place and his lineage, it might be assumed that Peter Gardner would have received his training in the career which was to bring him such renown at Dunmore Pottery, but this may well not be the case. It is curious that he should be omitted from the Census Returns in both 1851 and 1861, when he would have been about 17 and 27 years old respectively. This raises the question of where he was at those times. Wherever it was, it seems probable that he was undergoing training and work experience as a potter. The most obvious place to look would be just across the River Forth at Alloa, where his uncle, William Gardner, ran a sizeable pottery, but an examination of the Old Parish Registers by Robert Rankine has failed to produce any evidence of him there. Perhaps we should look elsewhere in Scotland, or in England; or even further afield, to the Continent. Without any definite lead to go on, it would be idle to speculate further.

Wherever he had been, Peter Gardner was back at Dunmore Pottery by the mid 1860s. Arnold Fleming in his standard book *Scottish Pottery* says: "Until 1860 it was rather a slow-going unenterprising concern, after which it blossomed out into much greater activity. Peter Gardiner [the family originally spelt their name with an 'i', but dropped it around 1825], a native of Alloa [incorrect], where his people had been potters for many years [true of his uncle William], is credited with this improvement, having about that date taken full possession of the works [improbable]".[16] That was not his sole occupation, however, for it must be remembered that Dunmore Pottery was located in an essentially rural setting, amid the fertile farmland of the Carse of Stirling. This situation attracted the attention of Professor Archer when writing a brief article on the state of the Scottish pottery industry in 1880: "The works are unique in one respect – they are situated in the middle of a farm in a neighbourhood quite rural, and to the passer-by give no very recognisable indication of their nature".[17] He is mistaken about this situation being unique, and also in his assertion that the Pottery was in an "unpromising locality" considering the abundance of raw materials which lay readily to hand, but there is no denying the farming connection. Indeed, at the end of the 18th century, Peter Gardiner (grandfather) was apparently referred to as a "farmer potter".[18] Half a century later, John Gardner (father) was recorded as following the same combination of employment, in the same order of priority, being listed as a "farmer & potter" in the 1851 Census Returns, and again as a "farmer and potter master" in 1861, with his spouse down as "farmer & potter's wife". This joint interest in both farming and potting may be regarded as a fairly normal feature of the pre-industrial era, but in the case of Dunmore it seems to have lasted right through the Pottery's productive life. For example, the Ordnance Survey Name Book for the parish of Airth described the complex of buildings in 1862 in the following fashion: "Pottery. A large Farmsteading, two storeys, slated and in good repair. It takes its name from an extensive Pottery Work connected with it. Property of the Earl of Dunmore, Dunmore Park, Airth". Although Peter Gardner himself is referred to only as a potter in the Census Returns, other evidence shows that the farming connection was maintained. In a legal tract of 1867, he is referred to as "Peter Gardner, Potter and Farmer at Dunmore Pottery, only son and heir of the deceased John Gardner, Pottery and Stoneware Manufacturer at Dunmore".[19] It was not just the Gardner family who were affected by this type of working practice. The Census Returns illustrate a similar merging of interests among the workforce, particularly the blurred distinction between a pottery labourer and an agricultural labourer in the 1861 Census (see Appendix A). The Valuation Rolls also illustrate this point; e.g. Andrew MacCowan, a sub-tenant of Peter Gardner, is listed as a ploughman in 1885, but as a packer (of pottery) in 1889, that latter term being confirmed by the 1891 Census, in which he is described as a "Pottery packer".

With the great potteries of the industrial era so thoroughly urbanised, it is easy to forget that the pre-industrial potteries had an essentially rural character. Even Delftfield, the first truly industrial pottery in Scotland, when founded in 1748 was located some little distance to the west of Glasgow, surrounded by fields. The old Scottish burghs, normally so keen to accommodate skilled craftsmen, did not offer a welcome to potters, probably because of the fire-risk which they posed due to the storage of combustible materials and the firing of their kilns. It is hardly surprising, then, that if the potters of those times were based in the countryside, away from the centres of population and the mass-markets which they presented, they could satisfy local needs by operating part-time, switching to the alternative occupation of agriculture on a seasonal

Figure 4

basis. Only a few of these pre-industrial rural potteries have been identified. One lay in the parish of Kelton in Kirkcudbrightshire, which was referred to in the *Statistical Account of Scotland* thus: "In the S.E. border of the parish there has anciently been a pottery…From this work, the farm in which it is situated has derived its name, *Potterland* ".[20] If it was regarded as ancient in 1793, when the account was published, it must surely have been pre-industrial, and indeed the scant evidence which has so far been discovered suggests that it was Medieval in date. The craft of potting there may have been over for centuries, but a vestige of that heritage lives on in the farm name (see Figure 4). In one sense, therefore, Dunmore Pottery was looking back to traditional ways, even in the time of Peter Gardner, but, by virtue of his vision and his application, he anticipated the craft pottery movement of the second half of the 20th century as he looked towards an exciting future.

Because Arnold Fleming suggests that Dunmore Pottery "blossomed out" under the management of Peter Gardner after 1860, it has come to be regarded that this change occurred very soon after that date. However, his father was still in charge of the works, being described as a master potter in the Census of 1861, while he himself is not even mentioned. Whether or not John Gardner went into retirement we do not know, but following his death on 23rd December 1866, Peter Gardner would have assumed full control if he had not done so already. This would indicate that the great era of potting at Dunmore started in 1867 (at the latest), but this is not borne out by newspaper reports and other evidence, which demonstrate that such a date is too early. One reason for the slow progress following the start of his period of tenure may have been the slump in value suffered by the Pottery and its associated farm land. The Valuation Rolls show that at the end of John Gardner's time, it had an annual rental value of £100, a figure

Figure 5

which it retained for the first full year of Peter Gardner being officially in charge, but in the following year, 1868, it fell dramatically to £29 10s. Having less rent to pay would no doubt have been welcomed, but the reasons for that may have had an adverse effect on any new enterprise. The true dawn of Dunmore's greatness under Peter Gardner occurred in 1874, when two events combined to bring it to the forefront of public attention. One was the attraction of noble and royal patronage; the other was connected with the display of farming implements at an agricultural show.

The key event in the launch of Dunmore pottery along the path to renown, and Peter Gardner to celebrity, occurred at the annual show of the Highland and Agricultural Society of Scotland (for badge, see Figure 5). In 1874, it was held at Inverness, and ran from 28th to 31st July. Amongst all the livestock on show, there was an exhibition of farm implements, and the organisers permitted other items of interest to the farming community to be included. It was here that 'Dunmore Nouveau' was revealed to an enthralled public. The first newspaper to pick up on the fact that something new and rather special was to be viewed here was the *Edinburgh Courant* of 29th July. It reported: "We may mention that yesterday the stand of Mr Jenkinson, of 10 Princes Street, Edinburgh, was largely frequented by ladies, who had a most attractive exhibition presented to their view," and after describing a display of glassware, it continued: "There is, however, another portion of it which possesses the characteristic of novelty. We refer to the exhibition of the Dunmore pottery ware". The key word here is 'novelty'. It would seem that Peter Gardner owed a debt of gratitude to Mr Jenkinson of Edinburgh for providing him with his first major public showcase, and although Dunmore was not mentioned by name, his stand at the show was advertised on the front page of *The Scotsman* on 28th July (see Figure 6). The Post Office Directories suggest that this man could have been A. Jenkinson of John Miller & Co., who first appeared in 1861. At the same time, a John Miller ran a "stone warehouse" (meaning a building which housed stoneware) at 19 Castle Street, Edinburgh, but not as part of a company.

HIGHLAND AND AGRICULTURAL
SOCIETY'S SHOW AT INVERNESS.

A. JENKINSON, China Merchant,
10 PRINCES STREET, Edinburgh,
Will Exhibit TABLE DECORATIONS, &c.,
At STAND No. 23.

Figure 6

A more likely candidate would be John Millar (spelt with an 'a') & Co., Potters to Her Majesty, who operated a china and glass warehouse at 2 South St Andrew Street. This would fit in with the royal and aristocratic patronage which Peter Gardner quickly established for his new wares. This same A. Jenkinson (his home address remains constant) went on to establish himself as a china merchant and glass manufacturer in 1872, based at 10 Princes Street, Edinburgh – the man who gave Peter Gardner his first public showing. If he had indeed been with John Millar & Co., he would no doubt have built up some influential contacts which would have been most useful to him in his new business, including the promotion of the 'novelty' ware now coming from Dunmore.

The curious feature about these new Dunmore products which were causing such interest was that they did not have the spectacular coloured glazes which characterise the output of the Pottery under Peter Gardner to such a large extent. Indeed, it seems that the glaze was not novel at all, according to the *Courant* reporter, who referred to "this ware, a revival of the old Rockingham manufacture…". Rockingham ware – not to be compared with the products of the English china factory of that name, which had ceased production in 1842 – had a heavy earthenware or stoneware body, treated with an all-over coating of thick, treacly brown glaze. It was much favoured by a number of Scottish potteries over quite a long period, especially for teapots. It seems to have continued under Peter Gardner (Fleming describes his range of teapots as including those with "the usual brown Rockingham glaze"), but it seems that this new Dunmore version was a little bit special, as the *Courant* described: "The articles have much the appearance of those made from common fire-clay, but they have a peculiar polish and very beautiful appearance." This suggests that it was not Rockingham ware at all, to which it probably bore no more than a very slight and superficial resemblance. The reporter clearly had a passing knowledge of ceramics, but may well have lacked the necessary degree of perception to make such a judgement. "Made from common fire-clay" is somewhat unlikely, unless perhaps for items of garden furniture; the phrase was perhaps chosen to indicate the use of a somewhat rougher clay than that employed by the earthenware factories of the period. "A peculiar polish" is not a ceramic term at all, and may well refer to an unusual form of glaze which had been fired to a highly glossy finish. "Very beautiful appearance" may be taken as indicating that the items under review had an artistic quality seldom encountered when dealing with the normal run of utility Rockingham ware. The type of product which typifies the first phrase of this 'new Dunmore' might be as represented on the cover of this booklet – the leaf-shaped dish is decorated with merging green and brown glazes which conform with the so-called 'autumn colours' that brought fame to Dunmore; they frequently appear in darker shades than shown here, which the untutored eye could readily confuse with Rockingham ware. The shape, too, is right for the period, and stands up to close comparison with a 'rustic' leaf-shaped dish produced by Charles Bellfield & Co. of Prestonpans, the design of which was registered in 1876.[21]

The other novel aspect of these Dunmore items was their general nature, which seems to have been somewhat removed from the mundane. The *Courant* gives a few examples: "The articles exhibited consist of afternoon tea-sets, garden seats, fern stands, flower stands, fruit dishes, taper stands, figures, &c., of exquisite design". This ties in, to some extent, with the Catalogue entry for Alexander Jenkinson of 10 Princes Street, Edinburgh, which listed five groups of exhibits (nos. 182-186) at Stand No. 22, the most likely-sounding being no. 183: "Garden Vases – Price from 12s. to £3" (p.13). The maker of Dunmore pottery gets due mention in the *Courant*: "It is manufactured, as its name indicates, on the Dunmore estate by Mr Gardner, one of the tenants". It is a little surprising that no mention is made of the support given by the Earl of Dunmore – but even more highly-placed patrons had already taken a fancy to Dunmore ware. The *Courant* notes that it is "much in request by the upper classes of the country…and has attracted the notice of His Royal Highness the Duke of Edinburgh, who has become a purchaser of some of the ware; and it has otherwise met with great favour from the aristocracy".

Undoubtedly the success of Dunmore Pottery was in no small measure due to its royal patronage. The connections it enjoyed with Queen Victoria and with the Prince of Wales (future King Edward VII) will be examined elsewhere in this booklet, but it seems appropriate at this juncture to underline that it had attracted the attention of *another* member of the royal family *before* it became famous following its launch at Inverness. This was Prince Alfred, Duke of Edinburgh (1844-1900), fourth child of Queen Victoria and younger brother of Edward, Prince of Wales. He was created Duke of Edinburgh in 1866. On the death of his paternal uncle, he became Duke of Saxe-Coburg & Gotha in 1893, and that is where he spent most of the remainder of his life. Interestingly, and of relevance to the Dunmore situation, he was active in encouraging the Duchy's industry and agriculture. The fact that he so quickly acquired some examples of Peter Gardner's new wares may well have encouraged other members of the aristocracy to do likewise, as indicated in the newspaper account, and would have been of great assistance in getting the 'new Dunmore' off to a flying start.

The fact that it really was new was emphasised in a report which appeared in *The Scotsman* of the day following the publication of the *Courant* article, 30th July 1874, though it was much briefer than that of the *Courant*. It began: "A new industry has been inaugurated on the estate of the Earl of Dunmore, Stirlingshire – namely, the manufacture of pottery". It does not describe it as Rockingham ware, though it comments: "The ware is brown, but it is extremely light."

That last observation means that it differed somewhat from traditional Rockingham ware in terms of weight, and emphasises the doubts expressed above about the validity of the use of this term in the *Courant* article. The report adds: "A large assortment of articles made at the Dunmore Pottery are exhibited here on Mr Jenkinson's stand", but gives no further details, except for a single mention which was made in the context of a fashion judgement: "Its appearance, say in a tea service, might at first sight seem *outré* [French, meaning 'beyond what is customary or proper'], but the fashion has, we believe, been set for it by its use in garden parties by the Duke and Duchess of Edinburgh". There is a suggestion of a double slight here – the notion that it was somewhat bizarre, and that it was only fit for outdoor use. It was, however, 'saved' by its royal patronage. It is interesting that both the Duke and the Duchess are mentioned. Prince Alfred had married

Figure 7

Marie Alexandrovna, daughter of the Emperor of Russia, at the Winter Palace in St Petersburg on 23rd January 1874, barely six months before the Highland Show at Inverness. If she had played a part in the acquisition of Dunmore articles for the royal household, then it underlines once more that such products did indeed represent a form of novelty at that time. (For a portrait photograph of the couple, see Figure 7).

The notice in *The Scotsman* makes one other rather curious comment, likening Dunmore ware to "the celebrated Valerie pattern of France", and suggesting that it was derived from it. Valerie was the name of one of the decorating studios of Limoges porcelain, which is not in the least like anything produced at Dunmore. However, this may not be what the *Scotsman* reporter meant at all. The previous day's *Courant* had noted that "Mr Jenkinson also shows various specimens of the 'Vallery' pottery" (as distinct from Dunmore), the two examples cited being plaques mounted on velvet, and ram's-head brackets. Although these are not mentioned in the exhibition Catalogue, the one of the following year included among Jenkinson's exhibits something called a 'Vallerio bracket'. Alternatively, there might be quite a different explanation to account for all this confusion. Perhaps the *Scotsman* reporter did not mean 'Vallery/Valerie' at all, but Vallauris, which, in its proper French pronunciation, sounds almost the same. This was a centre for ceramic production of long-standing, situated in the extreme south-east of France. It blossomed in the late 19th century, mainly due to the activities of the Massier family. Some of their products can indeed stand comparison with Dunmore ware, but most of them post-date 1874, and the supposed connection may be nothing more than a red herring.

Dragging along several days after the *Edinburgh Courant* and *The Scotsman* came the *Stirling Journal & Advertiser*, and considering that it was to an extent the local paper, it was none too pleased at the situation. It ran an article in the issue of 4th August under the headline "A NEW INDUSTRY – DUNMORE", in which it was scarcely able to contain its embarrassment, beginning: "It is curious, wonderfully curious, that we should have to go to Inverness to find out a new industry that is practiced at our own doors, and under our noses. Yet so it is. The new industry inaugurated by Lord Dunmore never came within our observation until now". This was obviously a source of irritation, and although wrapped up in polite phrasing, the critical comments which followed could hardly have been more pointed: "Whether the fault is his lordship's or ours we shall not pretend to say. But the fact is nevertheless potent that a manufactory of articles in clay, and generally of pottery ware, has been going on of which we in Stirlingshire knew nothing…We shall never forgive the Earl of Dunmore for causing us to go all the way to Inverness to find this secret out". If the novelty of these Dunmore products was not already demonstrated sufficiently, then it most certainly was by this tirade.

Once more, 'Rockingham' was the label attached to the wares on show: "Lord Dunmore has revived the old Rockingham manufacture which is so much prized by connoisseurs. Lord Dunmore has beaten the old Rockingham out of the field". This last observation confirms the aspect of novelty, though it is a pity that the reporter did not specify in what way the new differed from the old. Both the potter and his promoter get due mention: "The exhibition [of Dunmore ware] was striking, although it formed only a part of the goods shown by Mr Jenkinson of Edinburgh. The Dunmore portion was under the charge of Mr Gardiner [misspelt], who superintends the manufacture of the goods [making the point by using this phrase twice in the space of half a dozen lines]…and his taste and judgement is beyond all question". He was also revealed as having a keen sense of the marketing side of the business: "The young lady who superintended the sale did all in her power to make the goods attractive". Considering that the Highland Show drew large crowds over several days (then as now), Peter Gardner was clearly displaying his commercial acumen with this type of promotion.

The royal and noble patronage already received by Dunmore products did not escape the notice of the reporter: "His Royal highness the Duke of Edinburgh has become a large purchaser of the ware, [and] other aristocratic families have done the same thing". However, it would seem that this was not as elitist as might be assumed, for the anonymous Stirling journalist then proclaimed: "Let it be known that articles from this pottery can be obtained on easy terms [*i.e.* cheaply] by the meanest in the land. There is no reason why on old woman should infuse her tea in an old useless pot, when she can get a good and serviceable pot for little more than half the sum, and which will be the cheaper in the long run". Far from being the exclusive preserve of the highest echelons of society, the claim is here made that Dunmore ware was attractive to and affordable by *all* levels of society.

The *Stirling Journal* was clearly still somewhat piqued at being so late into print on this subject, "which we only discovered during a desultory stroll in the Show Yard at Inverness". It quoted fairly extensively from the *Edinburgh Courant*, "not that its opinion is better than ours, but that it was earlier on the field than we were", without further comment, and also from *The Scotsman*, though this drew a vitriolic response. The cause of its ire was the charge made against Dunmore products of being *outré*, which resulted in the following riposte from the *Stirling Journal*: "After this we fear that Lord Dunmore may shut his newborn potteries". If that may seem to be an over-reaction, the next comment was rather more measured: "The sneer is so visible as to do no harm". From there, the article petered out somewhat, but not before the rattled reporter had mistakenly called beautiful clay figures 'potsherds' (the term means pieces of broken pottery). The article concluded with the cryptic comment: "Keep away from Lillieshill, Lord Dunmore beats them all". This is a reference to Lillieshill Fireclay Works near Dunfermline, a dozen or so miles distant; they included garden furniture among their products, and so were rivals of Dunmore to an extent. At least the *Stirling Journal* gave some credit to the Earl (notwithstanding his supposed 'secrecy'), though perhaps too much, claiming that "Lord Dunmore, with the assistance of Mr Gardiner, has called into being" the new Dunmore products.

The reports of these three newspapers leave no doubt that the output of Dunmore Pottery in 1874 was dramatically different from what had been made there for many decades past, to such an extent that they were dismissive, perhaps even ignorant, of the basic wares which had been its mainstay for generations. The claim of secrecy regarding the change in production, if we allow that it is more than simply an over-dramatised reaction by a reporter who was peeved at being caught out, is hard to fathom. Perhaps Peter Gardner wished to launch his new lines, like some latter-day couturier, at a major public show which would attract intense interest from the

Press. Alternatively, it could have been due to the attitude of the Earl of Dunmore, who might have wanted these special new products which were being made on his estate to win the approval of royalty and the aristocracy before being presented to an audience further down the social scale.

Four days after the rather petulant article in the *Stirling Journal*, the other local newspaper, the *Falkirk Herald*, paid its tribute to the new Dunmore ware in its issue of 8th August, but in a much more relaxed fashion: "During a recent visit to the quiet little village of Airth, we had dinner served to us in earthenware vessels made in the neighbourhood. The colour and shape of these vessels was so unusual as greatly to attract our attention; and we observe that they have had a similar effect on visitors to the recent show of the Highland and Agricultural Society at Inverness". There follows a fairly full account of the Dunmore ware at the Show, which is lifted straight out of the *Edinburgh Courant* of 29th July (without acknowledgement). It is preluded, however, by a comment of considerable significance: "There the exhibition of Dunmore pottery ware created quite a sensation on account of its novelty." This hammers home the point that what was seen at Inverness was startlingly new. The other telling aspect of the *Falkirk Herald*'s account is the reference to colour, as well as shape, being so unusual; that is difficult to square with the notion of it all being Rockingham ware. At the same time, if Peter Gardner had been displaying his spectacular glazes in 1874, that surely would have drawn excited comment, even hyperbole, from the newspaper reporters, so we may safely assume that this amazing element of Dunmore production was yet to come.

Peter Gardner must have been delighted by the reception given to his new Dunmore ware at Inverness, and there is every likelihood that he would have continued to exhibit at succeeding Highland Shows. In the 1875 show at Glasgow, Alexander Jenkinson was there again, though once more the Catalogue did not specify Dunmore ware. Stand No. 32 displayed a range of goods (nos. 268-282) which included several possibilities, the most likely being garden vases (no. 269), conservatory vases and stands (no. 270), flower stands (no. 272), a jardinaire [*i.e.* jardinière] (no. 273), and dinner, dessert, tea, and breakfast services (nos. 277-280). Happily, the presence of Dunmore is confirmed by *The Scotsman* of 27th July: "Mr A. Jenkinson of Princes Street, Edinburgh, has, on one of the largest and most elegant stands in the yard…a series of handsome table decorations in Minton, Worcester, Sevres, Chelsea, and Dresden china. But perhaps the most important part of the stand is that devoted to the exhibition of a new Scottish industry – the valerie pottery made at Dunmore". Here 'valerie' is used as a generic term, without being given the dignity of an initial capital letter, and still no explanation is offered to justify its continued use.

The *Scotsman* report continues: "This manufacture was established by the Earl of Dunmore on his estate about eighteen months ago [*i.e.* very early in 1874], and during the past year a great advance has been made in the quality of articles produced. In addition to the brown glazed ware which became so fashionable, they have succeeded in securing various fine tints of green and blue". So, just a year after the creation of the 'new Dunmore', another breakthrough had been achieved by Peter Gardner with the introduction of colour, and the Pottery had truly entered the era in which its famous reputation would be secured. Only a brief mention was given by *The Scotsman* of the items on display: "rustic baskets for flowers, tea sets for garden parties, &c.", but it did add a piece of information of great significance, to the effect that these "designs have been furnished by the Countess of Dunmore, who with her noble husband, takes great interest in the pottery". It is thus evident that the Earl and Countess, in addition to supporting their tenant in his enterprise, were actively engaged in the process which gave form to his famous products. Unlike the previous year, *The Scotsman* was first to the story of Dunmore's new range, and when the *Edinburgh Courant* came out a day later, 28th July, it contented itself with a short mention: "A large variety of the well-known Dunmore pottery is on view", adding "we notice that at this pottery goods similar to those manufactured at the Valery works in France are now being produced". Considering the developments made at Dunmore, this would seem to be a reasonable comment, but the *Courant* columnist, in contrast to the effusive reaction given to Dunmore products in that newspaper a year earlier, was disappointingly brief in 1875, being rather more taken by Jenkinson's new haggis dish!

Having made his mark on the home front, Peter Gardner now set his sights on a very wide horizon, and became a player on the world stage. One of the most inspired and inspiring fields of development of the Victorian era was the international industrial exhibition, and many countries organised events of this nature during the later 19th century. The year 1876 marked the centennial of the United States of America, and Philadelphia, one of the key locations in the movement for independence, and home of the Liberty Bell, commemorated the occasion by staging such an exhibition under the auspices of the United States Centennial Commission. In the Catalogue we find, in the list of exhibitors, "Peter Gardner, Dunmore Pottery, Stirling N.B." (p.110). He was located at Stand No. 177 in the Ceramics Section, listed under Classes 210 and 213. These are defined as comprising "Stone china, for chemists, druggists, etc., earthenware, stoneware, faïence, etc." and "Porcelain for table and toilet use, and for decoration", respectively (p.151). The second description is hardly appropriate, and even more oddly it is the only Class in which Gardner is placed in the list of exhibitors. The Catalogue entry for the Philadelphia Exhibition reads thus:

> "**Gardner, Peter**, Dunmore Pottery, By Stirling, Scotland. Rockingham Teapots, Baskets, Vases, Tea Services, Jugs, and Dessert Ware" (p.155).

It would seem from this that what was exhibited represented the first phase of the 'new Dunmore' – Rockingham is mentioned, but any suggestion of colourful glazing is absent. The fact that the term Rockingham occurs in an official publication rather than a newspaper should not be taken as absolute confirmation that the goods so described certainly belonged to this type of ware, even if Gardner had written this description himself. There is no shortage of examples of well-known pottery firms using fundamental ceramic terms such as porcelain, earthenware, and stoneware, with a cavalier disregard for basic accuracy. In the above Catalogue entry, a lot depends on whether the epithet 'Rockingham' applies only to the teapots, in which case it is no doubt accurate, or to all of the various goods described, in which case its use may be questionable. It is interesting to note that Dunmore's immediate neighbour in the Exhibition, at Stand No. 176, was their closeish neighbour back in Scotland: W. & J.A. Bailey of the Alloa Pottery, just a couple of miles away across the River Forth. They were also exhibiting Rockingham teapots, along with their engraved table glass. Bailey's were able to boast that they had won a silver medal at the Paris Maritime Exhibition of 1875; Dunmore was destined to achieve a similar honour at Edinburgh a decade later. Peter Gardner's products were well received at Philadelphia, news of which drew excited comment back home. Under the heading "DUNMORE / POTTERY WARE", the *Alloa Journal* offered the following: "Dunmore people, not to say Alloa people, will be glad to learn that Mr Gardner, whose productions have rendered Dunmore to be known throughout the whole globe, has already sold the whole of his pottery ware at the Philadelphia Exhibition…Orders are pouring in, and no doubt Mr Gardner's world wide reputation is envied by his brothers in trade. So well it might".[22] Selling out within two months of the opening must have been a satisfying achievement. Although greatly appreciated by the visiting public, it would appear that Dunmore ware was not quite so highly regarded by those who dispensed awards to exhibitors. A pamphlet entitled 'Ceremony of the distribution of awards to exhibitors in the International Exhibition, 1876, Judges' hall, Wednesday September 27' (Philadelphia, 1876) merely names the dignitary who represented each country whose citizens were successful; a six-volume record of all the award-winning exhibitors was also compiled, but neither Peter Gardner nor Dunmore Pottery features there.

Even allowing for an understandable element of pride which may have been translated into journalese of the 'local lad makes good' variety, the claim made by the *Alloa Journal* is quite remarkable. Less than two years after the launch of the 'new Dunmore', it was "known throughout the whole globe", and had won for Peter Gardner "a world wide reputation". Meanwhile, back on the home front, things quietened down for a while. The novelty of Dunmore ware inevitably began to wear off, and in 1876, when the Highland Show was held in Aberdeen, *The Scotsman* merely noted that "The pretty Dunmore pottery, the manufacture of which was a couple of years ago commenced under the auspices of the Countess of Dunmore, is represented by a fine collection of useful and ornamental articles". Peter Gardner's promoter was still doing him proud, for *The Scotsman* reckoned that Alexander Jenkinson's stall "must prove to non-agriculturalists the most attractive stand on the Links". In 1877, when the show was in Edinburgh, *The Scotsman* did not mention Dunmore pottery at all. It is unlikely that Dunmore made an appearance at a Highland Show again during the 1870s, for Alexander Jenkinson was not in attendance at Dumfries in 1878 or at Perth in 1879.

A dramatic change occurred at the Highland Show of 1880 at Kelso. Jenkinson was back, and so was Peter Gardner – only this time, he had a stand of his own. The Catalogue lists "Peter Gardner, Dunmore Pottery, Stirling" at Stand No. 49, which had a considerable frontage of 32 feet (more than most). A wide variety of items were listed and priced (nos. 454-472), which might have come in different sizes, as each price is followed by the phrase "and upwards". They consisted of "Vases 9d., Baskets 9d., Leaves, Plates, &c. 6d., Afternoon Tea Sets 8s., Toy Tea Set 3s., Toilet Set 4s., Jugs 6d., Medallions 6d., Candlesticks 9d., Cheese Stands 3s., Butter Tubs 9d., Wall Brackets 3s., Kettles 2s.6d., Tea-pots 6d., Ornamental Flower Pots 1s., Garden Seats 15s., Desert [*i.e.* Dessert] Sets 10s., Lamps 15s., Spittoons, &c." (pp.28 and 29). Peter Gardner would certainly have wished to publicise his new independent display, and he took a front-page advertisement in *The Scotsman* on 26th July, the day before the show opened

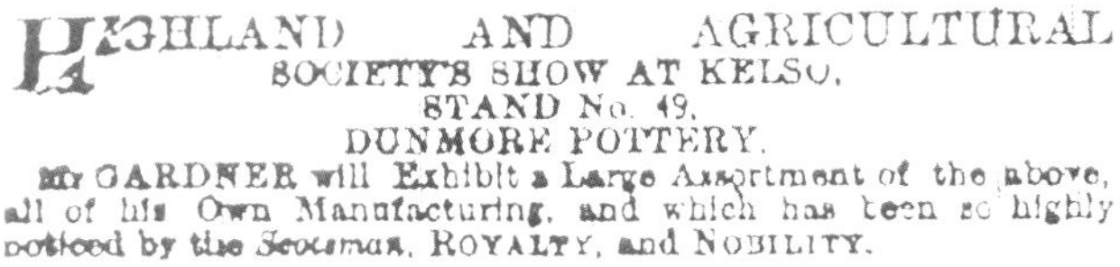
HIGHLAND AND AGRICULTURAL SOCIETY'S SHOW AT KELSO.
STAND No. 49.
DUNMORE POTTERY.
Mr GARDNER will Exhibit a Large Assortment of the above, all of his Own Manufacturing, and which has been so highly noticed by the *Scotsman*, ROYALTY, and NOBILITY.

Figure 8

(see Figure 8). Surprisingly, the newspaper omitted Dunmore from its customary extensive review of the Show; it did give a brief mention to the display of Alexander Jenkinson, though it noted that "fancy articles and table ware do not figure so largely as in some former shows". The reason may have been a shift in emphasis, for those displays "containing articles calculated to interest the housewife rather than the farmer" now concentrated on such items as washing and wringing appliances, sewing machines, and boot and shoe cleaners. *The Scotsman* seems to have given up reviewing the section on implements and other goods at this stage.

At the next Highland Show, Stirling 1881, Peter Gardner was back again. He was stationed at Stand No. 63 (of the same size as before), and the items on display (nos. 831-849) and their prices were exactly the same as the previous year. He did not attend the next two Shows, at Glasgow in 1882 and at Inverness in 1883, but he returned to the Highland Show when it was held in Edinburgh in the Society's centenary year, 1884, at Stand No. 113. On this occasion, the Dunmore display was somewhat reduced in size, having a frontage of 12 feet. (His immediate neighbour at Stand No. 112 was his erstwhile promoter Alexander Jenkinson, who commanded 50 feet.) The items on show (nos. 1642-1660) and their prices were exactly as they had been in 1880 and 1881. This event would seem to mark the end of Peter Gardner's participation in Highland Shows, for his name does not appear in the Catalogues for the remainder of the 19th century and beyond, and neither does that of Alexander Jenkinson. Perhaps the items which they purveyed were no longer considered appropriate to the interests of the farming community, and anyway other avenues of commercial promotion were gaining in popularity. Nevertheless, the Highland and Agricultural Society of Scotland had given Peter Gardner his first major breakthrough into the mass market where his pottery could be appreciated and acquired.

In the space of barely half a decade, Dunmore Pottery had gone from obscurity to widespread renown, thanks to the innovative work of Peter Gardner. In 1880, the *Art Journal* published a review of what it called "The Lesser Art Industries" (its principal interests being painting and sculpture). A small article on 'The Potteries of Scotland' was contributed by Professor Archer, almost half of which is devoted to Dunmore, which he describes as being "now well-known and much-admired". The *Scotsman* reviews of Peter Gardner's displays at Highland Shows have informed us that the 'new Dunmore' was launched in 1874, with coloured glazes other than Rockingham brown being introduced in 1875, but what of the mingling of colours which came to characterise Dunmore products, and which makes them so instantly recognisable today? It was not many years away, according to Professor Archer (though his supposed first phase was actually the third phase): "At first it [Dunmore pottery] was chiefly distinguished by its colour, a soft and pleasing neutral green, and other tints, especially rich deep brown and blue, and some with soft broad splashes of mixed tints".[23] That last phrase is most telling, for it is this feature above all which makes Dunmore ware so very special. However (and here we see a comparison with its famous cousin, Wemyss Ware), it was not colourful decoration but shape and form which had provided the basis of its reputation, as Archer indicates: "What has doubtless had the greatest effect in securing its well-deserved popularity is the classical style, or simple quaintness of shape, and its unobtrusive character. These are its highest qualities". These comments by Professor Archer are of interest and value, because unaccountably Dunmore Pottery was overlooked by the leading writer on ceramics during the Victorian era, Llewellynn Jewitt. It is absent from his standard work *The Ceramic Art of Great Britain* of 1878, by which time Dunmore was well-known, and the omission was not rectified when a new edition was published some five years later, Dunmore by then having achieved a wide degree of fame. It was only when a fresh edition, revised and expanded by Geoffrey Godden, was published in 1972 that Dunmore Pottery was given a paragraph. Its products were summarised there as being of "richly decorated useful earthenware".[24] Despite this, Dunmore Pottery was unaccountably omitted from the 1974 publication *Victorian Art Pottery* by E. Lloyd Thomas (which in other respects is an excellent book), even though there is no indication that this work was restricted to English potteries, and indeed the term 'British' is sometimes used when considering wares in their wider context. Comparisons can certainly be drawn between Dunmore and certain English art potteries of the period, such as the Bellevue Pottery of Frederick Mitchell at Rye which made 'Sussex Rustic Ware' in the period 1869 to 1875, and continued in somewhat similar vein for several decades after that. Also worthy of note in this respect are a linked group: the Linthorpe Pottery near Middlesbrough in Yorkshire, founded in 1879 and run by Henry Tooth until 1882; the Bretby Art Pottery (actually at Woodville, several miles away) in Derbyshire, established in 1883 with Henry Tooth and William Ault as partners; and Ault's own pottery, which he started at Swadlincote, just a mile away, in 1887. Some individual Dunmore items and production techniques are directly comparable with certain English art potteries, such as the three-legged toad (with Burmantoft's Pottery, on the outskirts of Leeds), and craquelure glazing (with the Sunflower Pottery, in Somerset); these topics are considered in their respective sections (nos. 30 and 27) when examining the text of the *Visit* booklet.

The novelty of this 'new' Dunmore ware was certainly attracting attention, as was noted by the Scotland correspondent of the *Pottery Gazette* in 1883 when considering the difference which then existed between pottery production on either side of the east-west divide: "One may be allowed to wonder why the well known energy and business capabilities of our Glasgow and west-country makers should actually appear dormant or moribund, as to the east-country houses may be credited the starting and developing of all the fresh wares and processes of late years".[25] Five factories are then mentioned, including that in Alloa and three in Kirkcaldy, but topping the list is "the Dunmore wares of Mr Gardner, Dunmore". Dunmore Pottery was clearly prospering. Peter Gardner took out an advertisement in the *Pottery Gazette Diary* in 1882 which began: "Mr Gardner begs to express gratitude for the patronage with which he has been so liberally favoured, and is increasingly enjoying. His Customers and the Public may be assured that no effort will be spared on his part to deserve their continued approbation and support".[26] Describing his venture with somewhat forthright immodesty as "this elegant and deservedly popular manufacture", he went on to quote extensively from the *Scotsman* review of his Highland Show display of seven years earlier, though interestingly he took care to omit the reference to the 'Valerie' pottery of France; perhaps he did not appreciate such comparisons being made. Three years later he took out another advertisement in the same journal under the heading "DUNMORE ART POTTERY" (see Figure 9), no doubt appreciating the value, in terms of both profit and status, of adopting such a soubriquet. The essential qualities of Dunmore ware are summed up in four words: "Artistic Shapes. Rich Colours". Claiming such a title was akin to joining a select club for Peter Gardner. Lloyd Thomas has nicely summarised what it means: "Art pottery was essentially a phenomenon of the last thirty years of the nineteenth century. During this period the prefix 'Art', with a capital 'A', had a special significance, for it was used to describe domestic furnishings that were deliberately intended to be artistically original and creative, rather than routine commercial products. In particular, it implied that an article was an individual expression of the talents of an artist-craftsman, in the manner of the Arts and Crafts movement, or that it conformed to the 'aesthetic' and intellectual, if less practical, ideals of the contemporary Art movement. According to this definition, Art pottery was not characterised by any particular shape, or type of decoration, as were articles in the Art Nouveau style at the end of the century, but more by the spirit in which it had been made. For this reason it was regarded, in its highest form, as a branch of the fine arts, to be ranked with painting and sculpture".[27] It is disappointing to find that this same author, in the same book, published a list of potteries known to have made Art wares prior to 1901, or which incorporated the words 'Art Pottery' in their business names, and yet he did not include Dunmore.[28] Even allowing the caveat that "within the space available it is obviously impossible to deal with all those potteries which claimed to produce Art wares",[29] the absence of Dunmore constitutes an unfortunate and significant omission.

DUNMORE ART POTTERY.
ARTISTIC SHAPES.   RICH COLOURS.
UNDER THE PATRONAGE OF THE EARL OF DUNMORE

The articles manufactured at the Dunmore Pottery include Vases, Afternoon Tea Sets, Garden Seats, Flower Pots, Dessert Plates, Leaves ; Mantelpiece, Dining-room, Drawing-room, and Toilet Table Ornaments, &c. &c., and are no less substantial than elegant, while they are inexpensive. The Ware is admirably adapted for Stalls at Bazaars, Prizes for Flower and all other Popular Competitions, &c.

PETER GARDNER, DUNMORE POTTERY, NEAR STIRLING, SCOTLAND.
SHOW ROOMS—51, PRINCES STREET, EDINBURGH ; ALSO ARCADE, STIRLING.

Figure 9

It might seem unrealistic, even unreasonable, for anyone to challenge the right of Dunmore to be included in the ranks of Art potteries, but it appears that it would not have found favour with the founding father of the Arts and Crafts movement, William Morris. According to Lloyd Thomas in his book *Victorian Art Pottery*, "although Morris had no first-hand experience of pottery manufacture, this did not prevent him from criticising the general state of pottery design as 'styleless anarchy', and he laid down five canons as a guide for good taste".[30] The first two of these, as summarised by Thomas, reflect in an adverse light upon the work of Peter Gardner:

"(i) No article should be moulded if it can be made by throwing on the wheel, or otherwise by hand". A fairly large percentage of Dunmore ware is moulded, a great deal of which could have been made by hand.

"(ii) Pottery should not be finished in the lathe". Contrast the sentiment expressed in that dictum with the opinion of the author of the *Visit* booklet, who considered that the thrown pots were "mere caricatures of graceful and beautiful shapes" until they had passed through "the hands of the artist" – and that was the turner, "standing before his lathe, making the superfluous clay fly before his clever fingers…proud of his machine and the wonders it worked".

It is improbable that William Morris had Dunmore ware (the products of a Scottish pottery) in mind when he formulated his five canons, as his views tended to be expressed in strongly Anglo-centric terms. It is unlikely that we shall ever know if Peter Gardner was aware of the pronouncements made by William Morris; perhaps, more pertinently, we should ask if it would have made any difference if he had. Probably not. That 1885 advertisement had him in good company, for also advertising alongside Dunmore were the likes of Tooth & Ault of Bretby Art Pottery ("rich and harmonious in colour, artistic in form and treatment"); Calvert & Lovatt, "Art and Stone Pottery Manufacturers" of Langley Mill Pottery near Nottingham; and the "Domestic Art Pottery" in Devonshire faïence and Aller Vale terra-cotta from Newton Abbott. This all helps to place Dunmore in a wider ceramic context.

The advertisement in the *Pottery Gazette Diary* states that there were Dunmore showrooms in Edinburgh and Stirling. It might be expected that by this date (1885), a showroom would also have been established in London (providing another comparison with Wemyss Ware, which utilised the premises of the well-known firm of Thomas Goode & Co. of South Audley Street, and often marked its ware accordingly). It has been reported that Dunmore appeared in a catalogue of C. Hindley & Sons of Oxford Street in 1880.[31] If so, this would seem to have been an odd arrangement, for Charles Hindley & Sons of 132, 133, and 134 Oxford Street are listed in the London Post Office Directories as "carpet manufacturers, importers of turkey carpets, furniture printers, upholsterers, cabinet makers & decorators". This was their description in 1875 when the 'new Dunmore' was launched, and it remained consistent all through the 1880s. It also seems curious that if Dunmore did have a special London stockist in 1885, that was not mentioned in the advertisement of that year which appeared in the *Pottery Gazette Diary*, a London-based publication.

Having seen Dunmore pottery enjoy a successful outing at the Philadelphia International Exhibition of 1876, Peter Gardner no doubt would have appreciated the value of the high-profile exposure which his wares received, and would have wished for more. He attended several other events of a similar nature, though no more overseas venues have as yet been noted. One of the highlights of his career was his participation in the Edinburgh International Exhibition of 1886, and the interest shown in the Dunmore wares on display there by Queen Victoria. (This topic is examined in some detail in Appendix C). There was scarcely time for Peter Gardner to draw breath before he was exhibiting again. The Edinburgh event closed on 31st October, and on 25th November Dunmore ware was once more on display, this time at the Glasgow Industrial Exhibition. This is confirmed in the Guide Book to the exhibition, though the relevant entry contains no details whatsoever. It merely records, at Stand no. 260:

"DUNMORE POTTERY CO." (p.41).

Such brevity is very disappointing, as most firms provided a general description of what they had on show, some at considerable length; nor did Dunmore have an advertisement in the Guide Book, though quite a number of their fellow exhibitors did, some taking the opportunity to mention and even to illustrate the prize medals which they had just been awarded at Edinburgh (and Peter Gardner had also been a medal winner there). Assuming that the catalogue entries were based upon information supplied by the exhibitors, it is hard to comprehend why Gardner was so coy on this occasion. There is every likelihood, given the short period of less than a month between the two exhibitions, that he would simply have packed and shipped his wares straight from one to the other, in which case the Edinburgh description could have been used unaltered. It is unlikely that his stall would have been any smaller, for the plan of the layout at Glasgow shows it to have been larger than many of the others. A further disappointment occurs regarding the Exhibition Review, for Dunmore was not among those firms selected for description, nor does it appear in the advertisements sections. However, we are provided with a glimpse of what was on show courtesy of a cartoon sketch (which will be discussed later; see Figure 73). It would seem that vases were predominant.

The Glasgow Industrial Exhibition ran through to the end of January 1887, and it may be in some ways regarded as a prelude for a hugely grander event which was staged in the following year. This was the Glasgow International Exhibition of 1888, which resulted in more acclaim for Peter Gardner, as the *Falkirk Herald* proudly reported: "Among the specimens of his many-coloured ware, which is chiefly in dark shades, there are to be found Dunmore pottery vases, afternoon tea sets, flower pots, dessert plates, leaves, mantelpiece, dining-room, drawing-room, and toilet table ornaments, pedestals, medallions, lamps, baskets of flowers, &c. Here we have all kinds of odd nick-nackets [trinkets], many of which would probably have delighted the heart of Sir Walter Scott, a bust of whom stands on a table alongside one of Burns. Flower pots in novel shapes and colours are noticeable. They are the same as shown in Edinburgh, where they were seen and admired by her Majesty the Queen, who purchased a number of the patterns. The other objects of interest in this stand are many".[32] Pottery and glass at the 1888 Exhibition were reviewed for the *Glasgow Herald* by James Paton, who was the superintendent of Glasgow's museum collections. His introductory remarks regarding the Scottish pottery industry were unduly pessimistic and unrealistically deprecating, and also contained some rank errors (*e.g.* Buchan of Portobello did not make salt-glazed stoneware – and an earlier article demonstrates that he knew very well what the process involved, yet he seems to have been unable to recognise the results). Matters improved, however, when he came to deal with the Dunmore section: "Mr Peter Gardner of Dunmore Pottery, Larbert, is a man who has made a name to himself and to his ware which is well deserved. Dunmore pottery is an excellent example of what can be done by judicious taste to give really artistic decoration by inexpensive processes to a cheap material. The products of Dunmore Pottery come in price within the means of the humblest cottager who wishes to ornament his 'room' mantleshelf. The beauty of Dunmore ware arises, firstly, out of the endless variety of form, sometimes graceful and classical, sometimes bizarre and grotesque, into which it is moulded, and next it is equally due to the brilliant colours of the glazes of which Mr Gardner possesses the secret. Painting forms no feature of the Dunmore pottery, and the moulded ornaments employed are rather large and effective than fine and minute. It is a class of ware primarily suited for garden and conservatory decoration; but that original purpose has been modified and developed, so that not only stands, vases, and pots for the ornamentation of apartments are made, but ware for table use also forms a feature in the productions of Dunmore. The glazes which are effectively employed in this pottery are both numerous and brilliant in character".[33]

It is not surprising that James Paton was enthusiastic about Dunmore, as he had already acquired a large quantity of its wares for the city collections which he administered. The circumstances of this donation are explained in a letter written in 1922 (and still preserved) by Arnold Fleming, author of the standard work on Scottish Pottery which was published in the following year, in which he appealed for assistance in his efforts to gather historical information (in this instance from Mr Buick of the Hilton Brick and Tile Works in Alloa, which also produced pottery in its early days). In it, Fleming comments: "There was also Mr Peter Gardiner [misspelt] of Dunmore. We [meaning himself and his father, Sir James Fleming, who had been intending to write such a book before his death] knew him well…Mr Gardner was very kind to me. We had a small Exhibition of Pottery in the People's Palace [Museum in] Glasgow & he lent a case of his ware which he ultimately gave to the Corporation".[34] (It would seem that Arnold Fleming is guilty of creating an anachronism here. The only donation of Dunmore pottery which Peter Gardner made to Glasgow Corporation was received in 1878 – all of twenty years before the purpose-built People's Palace Museum opened. The exhibition which he recalled was probably staged in the McLellan Galleries, founded in 1854, or possibly in Kelvingrove House, acquired in 1870.[35]) The records show that 87 items were accessioned in 1878, the source being "Peter Gardner, Dunmore Pottery, Airth Road Station". Each piece is described as an "Illustration of Rustic Pottery from Dunmore". As no purchase price is given, this would seem to have been a gift, and many of these pieces are still held today at Kelvingrove. A number of them are illustrated here: Figures C2, C15, C16, C17, C18, and C20. Another noteworthy donor was the daughter of Arnold Fleming, the author of the standard work on Scottish Pottery, who gave 18 pieces in 1937 which presumably formed part of her father's collection (though he was still alive at the time). A couple are illustrated here: Figures C13 and C23.

During the last two decades of the 19th century, Peter Gardner continued to develop a staggering array of weird and wonderful shapes (a detailed discussion of which is beyond the scope of this booklet). While the glaze effect remained important, it was often the actual object, decorated in a single-colour glaze, which became the main attraction. The artistic sources were very varied, with Chinese influence often apparent, event to the extent of replicating Chinese objects. Above all, Peter Gardner was a skilled potter and a true ceramic artist. This is wonderfully demonstrated by a loop-handled bowl, some 5½ inches high, which reveals four different methods in its making: the basic bowl is thrown on the wheel, the handle is composed of extruded strands which have been intertwined by hand, the decorative elements which secure the handle to the body have been moulded, and the scalloped rim was created by cutting with a sharp implement (see Figure C21). A little masterpiece. Some other examples of his work are anything but little, such as a double-gourd vase with a textured body which is all of 22 inches high (see Figure C29). Indeed, special pieces of Dunmore abound, like the spectacular plaque, 22 inches in diameter, featuring a portrait of Marie de' Medici.[36] (Does the coincidence of dimensions indicate the maximum size of pot which the kiln could accommodate?) An indication of the skill factor involved is given in an appraisal by Barbara Davidson, who runs a modern pottery at Larbert: "Drawing in a pot to a very thin neck is one of the most difficult things to do on a wheel", yet this is a fairly common feature of Dunmore products (see Figure 31 top right, and Figure C18). Peter Gardner had an ally in his raw material, for she adds: "It shows how plastic and workable the clay was".[37] This is amply demonstrated by his liking for creating simulated wicker-work (see Figure C13). Such a technique was noted by Arnold Fleming during his visit to Dunmore Pottery: "Another characteristic style was the basket or wicker work, formed by weaving strands of clay, squeezed out of a squeezing box or press, in style similar to Leeds Pottery".[38] An example of Gardner's technical capability to produce complex items may be seen in the weaver bird and its nest (see Figure C19); likewise the multi-part vase cluster (see Figure C20). The name of Peter Gardner tends to be used almost synonymously with Dunmore Pottery, which is hardly surprising, for without his inspiration and enthusiasm, the name of Dunmore would not have risen to such eminence in the art pottery world. However, it should be remembered that one person can scarcely run a pottery of industrial scale single-handed, and his team of workers deserve some credit for the part they played. The Census Returns yield over fifty of their names (see Appendix A).

The success of Dunmore Pottery allowed Peter Gardner to build up a considerable holding of property in the area. This was not a new venture for the family, as his father John had also been active in similar undertakings. The Sasine Registers show that between 1851 and 1864, John Gardner (who is usually described as "Potter and Stoneware Manufacturer") was involved in six property transactions, but this was more than matched by his son. Starting in 1879, Peter Gardner made a substantial number of land purchases in the course of the next twenty years, acquiring these properties from various local tradesmen *e.g.* John Young, china merchant in Falkirk;[39] John Graham, formerly grocer in Falkirk;[40] Catherine Black, widow of David Buchanan, painter in Falkirk;[41] and James Heugh, baker in Airth.[42] Despite what must have been a considerable financial outlay, Gardner was still able to lend money *e.g.* £1500 to James Haddow, merchant in Falkirk, with more property put up as security which it took seven years to redeem.[43] He clearly possessed sound business acumen.

Near the end of his days, Peter Gardner erected a substantial building in Airth, consisting of a shop and six dwellings, which he rented out. The tenant was a grocer name Alexander McLuckie. Although the outlay was doubtless considerable, the annual rent provided a substantial return. In 1901, the grocer's shop was in the name of Annie McCulloch (rent £18), while the houses (rent £6 or £7) were occupied by a seaman, a dress-maker, a miner, and two labourers, (one being empty), which yielded a rental of £49 that year. This property became known as Gardner's Buildings, situated (in the Valuation Rolls) between Netherby Villa and Halls of Airth. (After Peter Gardner's death, his sister Mrs Helen Boyd of Westfield, by Airth, became the proprietor. Alexander McLuckie ran the grocer's shop himself until it was acquired in 1910 by William Mitchell, a butcher. Most of the tenants of the houses were miners, with a few less common trades, such as a moss cutter and a fruit grower. The shop was ultimately taken over by the Alloa Co-operative Society Ltd.)

Having been at the top of his game for around a quarter of a century, Peter Gardner began to slow down around 1900 as his health started to deteriorate. He died where he had been born, at Dunmore Pottery, on 1ˢᵗ March 1902, after a fairly prolonged illness. His obituary recorded that "though of an apparently robust constitution, [he] had been ailing for a considerable period, and for some time his illness completely confined him to the house". An obit notice appeared in *The Scotsman* on 4ᵗʰ March, with lengthy obituaries (the same text) being published in the *Falkirk Herald* on the 5ᵗʰ and in the *Stirling Journal & Advertiser* on the 7ᵗʰ. He was described therein as "a genial, shrewd, active, and level-headed man…Mr Gardner's hospitable nature and frank and genial disposition won him many friends". Tribute was paid to the manner in which he had developed the works: "The late Mr Gardner succeeded his father in the well-known and old-established pottery business at Dunmore…he succeeded in so extending the business that Dunmore Pottery ware was soon known all over the country, and was regarded as the most superior of its class…The articles manufactured embraced a variety of goods, some of which were extremely pretty and unique".

Nor surprisingly, mention was made of the special room at Dunmore Pottery House: "A good many years ago, he fitted up at the entrance to his works a drawing-room, which was beautifully appointed with Dunmore pottery ware. His works were every summer visited by people from

Figure 10

far and near, whom he delighted to welcome. In no part of his premises was he more interested than in the drawing-room referred to, and in it visitors viewed some of the finest productions of the potter's art". It is clear that the work involved in running Dunmore Pottery occupied most of Peter Gardner's time: "Throughout his life he devoted himself almost entirely to his own business, and he took no part in the administration of public affairs. He was, however, an elder in the Airth Parish Church, in the affairs of which he took a deep interest". As the Sabbath fell the day after his death, it is hardly surprising that reference should have been made from the pulpit concerning that sad event by the minister, the Rev. Frederic Hendry. Having only been appointed to Airth in 1900, he had to admit that "a longer acquaintance will perhaps enable many of you to form a juster impression of what he was than I can possibly do," but he added: "to everyone it was plain that he was a large-hearted, kindly, homely, bright-tempered man, ready to play his part, and to meet in a generous spirit every call made upon him…In recent interviews with him nothing struck me more than the extraordinary benevolence of spirit he displayed, his readiness to see good in everything and everybody."

Peter Gardner was buried under a handsome tombstone in Airth Kirkyard (see Figure 10), though it was erected not for him but for his father (in which case he was probably responsible for its erection). In all, it commemorates six people – John Gardner and his wife, and Peter Gardner and three of his sisters. The inscription is still reasonably legible (see Figure 11), but for ease of reading it has been copied out.

SACRED
TO
THE MEMORY OF
JOHN GARDNER
WHO DIED 23[D] DEC[R] 1866
AGED 68 YEARS
HIS ELDEST DAUGHTER **JANET**
WHO DIED 13TH SEP[R] 1838
AGED 8 YEARS
HELEN CATHIE
HIS WIFE WHO DIED
17TH AUGUST 1878
AGED 78 YEARS
ALSO
HIS DAUGHTER **MARGARET**
WHO DIED 17TH FEBRUARY 1885
ALSO
HIS SON **PETER** WHO DIED
AT **DUNMORE POTTERY**
1ST MARCH 1902
AGED 66 YEARS
ALSO HIS DAUGHTER
ANNE GARDNER WHO DIED
8TH NOV[R] 1915 AGED 75 YEARS

Figure 11

Curiously, the age given on the tombstone (and also in the obituary) for Peter Gardner is incorrect; born June 1834 and died March 1902 means that he had attained the age of 67 years. On 1st March 2002, the exact centenary of the death of Peter Gardner, a small group of enthusiasts, most clutching an item or two of Dunmore ware, assembled in Airth Kirkyard. After a couple of readings had been delivered, a wreath was laid on the grave. (Figure C29 shows the author with his prize Dunmore pot beside the last resting place of Peter Gardner.)

The minister mentioned that "from the time of my coming to Airth, Mr Gardner was in failing health", confirming that by 1900 Dunmore Pottery was on the decline. This is reflected in the Valuation Rolls. In that year, of the six houses situated at the Pottery, two were occupied by potters (Thomas Harrison and John Wright), two by labourers (possibly agricultural, possibly at the Pottery, most likely a combination of the two), and two lay empty. Following Peter Gardner's death, it seems as if the Pottery contracted further, for by then there were only three houses. The tenant was Thomas Harrison, who sublet them – two to miners, while the third lay vacant. This exodus of potters must have been felt severely at the works; they did not move to Airth or elsewhere in the parish, and so it would appear that they left Dunmore Pottery altogether to ply their trade elsewhere.

The demise of Peter Gardner did not end pottery production at Dunmore. Exactly six months later, it was announced in the *Falkirk Herald* that "This old-established business, so long and so successfully carried on by the late Mr Peter Gardner, has been let to his cousin, Mr R. B. Henderson, Falkirk, on a 21 years' lease, by the proprietors, the executors of the late Mr Claud Hamilton, Dunmore Park" (the Earl of Dunmore having lost control of the estate some years before). Then came the good news and the bad news: "It is Mr Henderson's intention to keep on the workers [those who remained] formerly employed by Mr Gardner in the business, and also to introduce to a certain extent machinery to replace hand labour, and so enable him to compete more successfully with more up-to-date firms".[44] Machine-made pottery, for all the commercial advantages it could offer, was not Peter Gardner's style. An up-beat advertisement was issued in 1905 which was very strong on interacting with the public: "always Open to Visitors…Inspection Invited…Tea and Aerated Waters may be had" (see Figure 12). Without the magic touch of Peter Gardner, however, long-term success could not be achieved, and about a decade later the great Dunmore kiln belched it last cloud of black smoke.

Of the various qualities of character mentioned in Peter Gardner's anonymous obituary and pulpit tribute, one is notable by its omission, and that is humour. This wont was corrected by Arnold Fleming when dealing with Dunmore Pottery in his standard work: "Before closing the subject of Dunmore I should like to add a little more about Gardner himself. A tall handsome man of jovial disposition, he was at heart an artist, and to visit him was always a delight, as he was invariably in the middle of some wonderful scheme for decorating his ware…He also took a keen interest in his garden, and delighted in showing his guests the quaint grotesque pottery figures and coloured glazed hens and dogs peeping out from under the shrubs and flowers in all sorts of cunningly-contrived nooks, and no-one enjoyed the surprise and occasional start of the visitor at those unexpected appearances more than himself ".[45] It is noteworthy that Fleming should devote so much detail to Peter Gardner. He was, after all, not a historian but a practical potter, and what he lacked in historical perspicacity he made up for in his knowledge of potting techniques and the potters themselves. Indicative of the high regard in which he held Gardner is the relatively lengthy description which he was accorded, being more extensive than that of any other potter in his book. Perhaps the last word should come from his obituary: "Mr Gardner took a great deal of pride in the kind of work produced at his Pottery" – a marvellously understated sentiment which is clearly evident in every one of the thousands of pieces of Dunmore pottery which happily still exist today.

DUNMORE POTTERY. by LARBERT,
is always Open to Visitors.
Beautiful Selection of WARE suitable for PRESENTS
and BAZAARS or WEDDING PRESENTS.
INSPECTION INVITED.
TEA and AERATED WATERS may be had.

Figure 12

LADY DUNMORE BOWL.

Figure 13

The sketch shows an interestingly-designed bowl in the shape of a ring-handled cauldron, standing on three upcurled feet, and moulded with an encircling band of Greek key pattern. The upper portion has been pierced by a series of narrow apertures, each section of clay being cut out by hand using a sharp implement, which suggests that the function of this item was to act as a pot-pourri; the fragrance of the dried petals which it contained could waft out through the slits (see Figure 13; also Figures 43 and C5 for the real object). In addition to achieving the accolade of featuring on the Frontispiece, a sketch of this bowl also appears in the text of the *Visit* booklet. In each instance, it bears the caption "Lady Dunmore Bowl". This is a reference to Lady Catherine, the Dowager Countess of Dunmore, who did much to assist Peter Gardner in his endeavours, as will be discussed later.

(III)   **Depots:**
22A Renfield Street, Glasgow
18A George Street, Edinburgh

It is evident that the popularity of Dunmore ware prompted Peter Gardner to open depots in Scotland's two major cities to promote and more readily market his products. He no doubt felt that it would be commercially advantageous to do so, as well as gaining a degree of kudos. However, the concept of a Dunmore Depot was not new to him, because he had already established one in Stirling. The earliest mention so far discovered appears in the Stirling Directory of 1882 (covering the year 1881-82), when Duncan's Glass and China Warehouse advertised that they were also a "Depot for the Celebrated Dunmore Pottery" (see Figure 14). We can be reasonably sure that Peter Gardner was responsible for this innovation, for when the same firm had advertised in the Stirling Directory of 1866 (the year his father died), it then being under Archibald Duncan rather than Peter Duncan, no mention was made of Dunmore ware. The Pottery itself rarely appears in these Directories, as they are usually confined to the town of Stirling, sometimes including a group of neighbouring townships, and so it is only when Stirlingshire is treated as a

Figure 14

county that the name makes an appearance, *e.g.* in 1893, when there was a separate entry for Airth and Neighbourhood. Under 'Miscellaneous', we have "Earthenware Manufacturer – Peter Gardner, Dunmore",[46] (notwithstanding that, in local terms, the Pottery was a considerable distance from Dunmore), though with no further detail.

The 1882 Directory which spoke of "the Celebrated Dunmore Pottery" was compiled in May of that year, and within a few months a major change had taken place regarding the marketing of Dunmore pottery in Stirling. In August of that year, a fancy fair was held in the Smith Institute to raise money to acquire an organ for the Albert Halls nearby. An extraordinary booklet accompanied it, published by Robert Shearer, a local bookseller, entitled *Officiale Hand Boke*

DUNMORE POTTERY, by STIRLING

PETER GARDNER

BEGS respectfully to intimate that he has opened a Depôt for the Dunmore Pottery in the Stirling Arcade, where Specimens of the Articles will be on Sale and Orders taken. Dunmore Pottery is about six miles from Stirling by road, on the Dunmore Estate, and within a short distance of Dunmore House, one of the Seats of the Earl of Dunmore.

Mr GARDNER will be glad to show the Works to visitors who are interested in the manufacture. The articles manufactured at the Dunmore Pottery include Vases, Afternoon Tea Sets, Garden Seats, Flower Pots, Dessert Plates, Leaves; Mantlepiece, Dining-room, Drawing-room, and Toilet Table Ornaments, &c., &c., and are no less substantial than elegant, while they are inexpensive. The Ware is admirably adapted for Stalls at Bazaars, Prizes for Flower and all other Popular Competitions, &c.

DEPOT—ARCADE, STIRLING.

Figure 15

[also known as the *Vision* on the cover] *of Ye Strivelin* [an archaic rendering of Stirling] *Fancye Fayre*. Getting past the quite amazing title page is the work of more than a moment; the reward within is a full-page advertisement for Dunmore Pottery (see Figure 15). In it, Peter Gardner announced that he had opened a depot for his products in the Stirling Arcade, listing a range of articles for sale, and, with a flair for promotion which seems typical of the man, declaring that they are "no less substantial than elegant, while they are inexpensive". He also indicated that he "will be glad to show the Works to visitors who are interested in the manufacture", hence the author of the *Visit* booklet would have experienced no difficulty in arranging for a tour of the Pottery. Most extraordinary of all is that the huge capital D of Dunmore Pottery is crammed with sketches of actual items which were made there! There are thirteen in all, jugs being a favourite. The two items in the bottom left of the D are illustrated in this booklet (see Figures C13 and C14). The artist may possibly be the person credited on the title page, "Master Drekab, Ye Drawing Man", though this would appear to be a pseudonym. However, writing 'Drekab' backwards produces 'Bakerd', which looks more like a name if it is rendered 'Baker D'. The Stirling Directory for that year does not list anyone called D. Baker, but there is a Baker, and he is well qualified to be the mystery artist: Leonard Baker, Board of Trade art master, at 22 Albert Place (fl.1865-1910). He was noted for his paintings of local views, and was generally known as the drawing master at Stirling High School. Another possibility is Edmund Baker (fl.1880-1910), who was also a Stirling artist who painted local views. With regard to the initial letter D before Baker, it may be more than a coincidence that both of these men's forenames end with this letter.

Promoting his wares well in Stirling was clearly good for business, but Peter Gardner had larger targets in mind, and he set his sights high with the establishment of depots in Glasgow and Edinburgh. It may be noted that both the locations which were chosen were as well known for their financial as their commercial operations. Neither depot was to survive for long, however, and the Post Office Directories for the two cities can supply fairly accurate dates for these ventures.

With regard to Glasgow, we have:
1887   Dunmore Pottery Depot, 22A Renfield Street
1888   the same, and also
            Peter Gardner, Dunmore Pottery; warehouse, 22A Renfield Street

The Dunmore Pottery Depot occupied basement premises; No. 22, from pavement level upwards, supported nine tenants in 1887 representing a considerable range of interests, with solicitors and stockbrokers well to the fore. Two of these tenants could possibly be of relevance here. One was David Miller & Co., turkey red and fancy yarn dyers, being the office of the Clydesdale Dye Works at Rutherglen, with Archibald Robertson in charge. Could there be a connection, considering the spectacular colour effects achieved by some of the Dunmore glazes, either in terms of inspiration, or even (if practical) the supply of ingredients? The other tenant was the Art Union of Glasgow, under the direction of James Spence, and also its secretary, a chartered accountant named McLean Brodie. Such an organisation can hardly have been unaware that they had the celebrated Peter Gardner as a neighbour, and it may be wondered if that might even have been a factor in his choice of premises. David Miller & Co. remained at No. 22 during the short tenure of the Dunmore Pottery Depot, though the Art Union of Glasgow left after the first year. Disappointingly, after only a couple of years, the Depot closed. It may not have been commercially viable, or perhaps it fell victim to new technology, because in 1889 No. 22A was occupied by the Bar-Lock Typewriter Co. and by W. J. Richardson & Co., manufacturers and importers of "office labour-saving devices" – typewriters, cyclostyle copying apparatus, and the like.

With regard to Edinburgh, we have:

1886	Peter Gardner (*Dunmore Pottery*), 32 Castle Street
1887	no entry
1888	Peter Gardner, Dunmore Pottery Depot, 18A George Street
1889	the same
1890	do. (the last year)

Peter Gardner had already established his presence in the Capital, sharing showrooms at 51 Princes Street in 1885 (see Figure 9). This might well have been when these premises were vacant of a long-term leasee – they are not listed at all in the Post Office Directories of 1884 and 1885, and by 1886 they were occupied by John Redfern & Sons, ladies' tailors. The first address for the Dunmore Pottery Depot listed in the Directories is 32 Castle Street. This was shared by two other tenants: William Fraser, the deputy keeper of the Records of Scotland, and Richard Gravett, a butcher. When the latter moved there from his previous premises at 12 East Register Street in 1883, he chose to give his new establishment the somewhat grandiose name of the Royal Emporium (and although it is not listed, it is referred to as such in advertisements in the Directories of 1884, 1885, and 1886; see Figure 16). This explains the curious address which appears on miniature bowls which Gardner used as a promotional gimmick to boost sales (see Figure 17; actual size). They bear relief Gothic script which reads "Dunmore Pottery / Depot Royal Emporium / 34 Castle Street Edinr." (see Figure 18; actual size). This may be more intelligibly rendered as "Dunmore Pottery Depot, Royal Emporium, 34 Castle Street,

ESTABLISHED UPWARDS OF HALF A CENTURY.

RICHARD GRAVETT,
BUTCHER
(Formerly of 52 Hanover Street, and late of 12 East Register Street).

ROYAL EMPORIUM, 32 CASTLE STREET.

RICHARD GRAVETT, in removing from 12 East Register Street, has secured those Central Premises, Royal Emporium, 32 Castle Street, and he trusts, by keeping a first-class article (as he has hitherto done) in both Home Bred and Home-Fed Ox Beef and Wedder Mutton, Lamb, Veal, and Pork, and by strict attention to business, and moderate prices, to merit a continuance of the public patronage so favourably bestowed upon him in former years.

BEEF AND PORK SAUSAGES, CORNED BEEF, PICKLED TONGUES, SALT ROUNDS.

Town and Country Orders punctually attended to.

As the Subscriber would like always to have a clear Shop—*Cut Pieces at a Discount.*

Figure 16

Edinburgh". These bowls must have been made in considerable numbers, for they are not all that uncommon today, occurring in dark green, deep red (*sang de boeuf*), ochre, and even fawn bisqueware. It is amusing to reflect that their proud owners may not be aware that the grand-sounding Royal Emporium was actually a butcher's shop! No such bowls are known to have been produced for either the Stirling or the Glasgow depots. (This style of script, incidentally, was favoured at Dunmore for adding inscriptions to items such as teapots. The earliest date so far recorded is 1880, though most belong to the post-1902 period. The inscriptions may comprise a personal name, a place-name, or a motto, and in that respect are comparable with the teapots produced at the Cumnock Pottery in Ayrshire about the same time.)

Figure 17

Keenly-aware readers may have detected that there is a discrepancy between the Directories and the advertising bowls in respect of the Castle Street address, the former giving it as No. 32 and the latter as No. 34. A facile solution would be to suggest that Gardner simply eased himself into the adjoining premises, but the problem is that they were not adjoining – they were separated by the considerable width of George Street. Whatever the precise nature of the circumstances, it lasted barely a year, for in 1887 Richard Gravett moved again, to 19 Broughton Street, taking neither the Royal Emporium name nor Peter Gardner with him. Only William Fraser remained at 32 Castle Street in that year, and it would appear that Gardner was left without an Edinburgh depot for a year or so.

However, the venture reappears in the following year's Directory, Peter Gardner re-establishing the Dunmore Pottery Depot at 18A George Street. This was a well-known address, and a potentially advantageous one for Peter Gardner, as No. 18 was occupied by Dowell's Auction Rooms (or, as they were officially known, "Dowell's Rooms for the sale of heritable and moveable property by auction"). Five auctioneers are listed there in 1888: James Dowell, Alexander

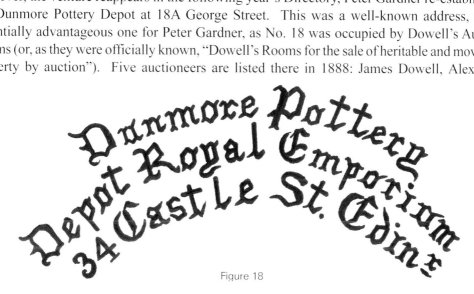

Figure 18

Dowell, Charles Munro, David Peters, and William Wilkie. Walter Brown was also part of the firm there. As auctions are not primarily about selling new goods, it cannot be assumed that any of these men actually put Dunmore ware under the hammer, but at the same time it is difficult to reject the notion that Gardner would have taken advantage of his locational link with Dowell's in some way which would have been to his commercial benefit. Such a suggestion is reinforced by the altered inscription which appeared on his miniature advertising bowls: "Dunmore Pottery / Depot 18 George Street / Edinburgh". Giving the address as No. 8 rather than No. 18A seems unlikely to have been a mistake. Sharing the basement quarters with Gardner were Thomas Carfrae, a stationer at No. 18B, while at No. 18C was The A. C. Thomson Company of Glasgow, makers of rubber stamps, office printing presses, type-writing machines, etc., Samuel McLean being in charge of their Edinburgh branch. It does not appear that his immediate neighbours would have had any significant effect upon the working practices of Peter Gardner, although the activities of The Thomson Company present uncomfortable parallels with the situation regarding the Dunmore Pottery Depot in Glasgow at precisely the same time. The Edinburgh Depot lasted a little longer, but it too had gone by the end of the decade.

As well as providing an insight into Peter Gardner's commercial activities, the reference to the two Dunmore Pottery Depots is of great assistance in dating the booklet *A Visit to Dunmore Pottery*, by virtue of the information contained in the annual Post Office Directories. It must be remembered, however, that the year covered by each issue is not a calendar year. Thus the issue published in 1886, for example, which carries the dates 1886-87 on its spine and its title page, actually covers twelve months spanning 1885-86, with a distinct bias in favour of the earlier year. With that proviso, we can ascertain the maximum time-period when the Dunmore Pottery Depots were operating in the two cities – Glasgow: 1886-89, and Edinburgh (second address): 1887-91. Taken together, we get the tighter date of 1887 x 89 for the booklet. This can be narrowed down even further, because the booklet refers to the Edinburgh International Exhibition of 1886, at which Dunmore ware was on display, but not to the Glasgow International Exhibition of 1888, where Dunmore ware was also featured. The booklet may therefore be dated to 1887 or thereby.

Proclamation in the Booklet

DUNMORE POTTERY.

————•————

Mr Gardner, in expressing gratitude for the patronage with which he has been so liberally favoured, begs to state that the public can be supplied with the " Real Dunmore " (Stamped), in either large quantities for Bazaars, &c, or small lots suitable for Presents, &c.

The Dunmore Pottery is admirably adapted for Stalls at Bazaars, &c.

A great many of the Patterns have been furnished by the Earl and Countess and Dowager Countess of Dunmore, and have secured the distinguished patronage of Her Most Gracious Majesty the Queen, and very many of the Nobility.

Figure 19

The expression 'proclamation' is used here, for want of a better term, to denote what appears to be a sort of preface which is delivered in a somewhat trumpeting fashion. There are two main points to note: the importance of a stamped mark signifying that any item bearing it is a genuine piece of Dunmore ware; and the regal and noble patronage enjoyed by Dunmore Pottery. The first of these points struck me as being of crucial interest when I first read the *Visit* booklet in 1975, and prompted me to compose a short article called 'On the importance of being marked....'.[47]

Marking

The application of a pottery maker's mark is a comparatively late feature of ceramic production, for in pre-industrial times most wares would have been sold, or bartered, within the locality where they had been made. The element of competition only came to the fore when factories began mass-producing similar wares, and distributing them widely. Nevertheless, transfer-printed ware of the late 18th and early 19th century not uncommonly bore the name of the pattern but not of the maker, and it was only when competition became keener with the rise of major factories, and distribution became wider thanks to an ever-expanding railway network, that manufacturers began to appreciate the value of identifying their wares in order to secure repeat orders from their dealers and other customers. Rather different was the situation of these potteries which specialised in lines not in general production; here the purpose of marking was to issue a declaration of authenticity, and to guide those lacking somewhat in perception away from cheaper (and doubtless inferior) imitations. These factories had to make a special effort, though, for it would have been unlikely for such firms to employ the transfer-printed method of decoration, and therefore there would be no handy corner of a copper plate for an engraver to create such a mark, which could then be readily applied to the bisque-fired wares. Instead, the name would have to be laboriously written by hand, using brush or stylus, or with greater facility be stamped on, the impression of a metal die being the generally-favoured technique. Incised or impressed marks had to be applied at the leather-hard stage; after firing, such marks could not be added to or altered in any way.

Of the two situations mentioned above, Dunmore Pottery would fall into the latter category. By referring to "Real Dunmore (Stamped)", Gardner might just as well have said "none genuine unless bearing the Dunmore stamp". It almost sounds as if he was concerned about the activities of imitators, and while a certain similarity may be detected in some of the shapes and glazes produced by the likes of Bailey at Alloa and Bellfield at Prestonpans at approximately the same time, Dunmore products are normally so distinctive as to be unmistakeable. Perhaps he was more worried by certain Continental lines of production; some French wares bear more than a passing resemblance to Dunmore. That having been said, it is clear that Peter Gardner, having established a renowned name and a lucrative trade, would have been most unwilling to see it threatened in any way by rivals attempting to emulate his highly distinctive wares. The implication of that key phrase regarding "Real Dunmore", verified by an impressed mark, is that there were similar goods on the market purporting to be the 'genuine product' *i.e.* quasi-Dunmore ware, or at least threatening to be mistaken for it. Gardner's statement implies that *all* Dunmore ware carries an impressed mark, and it is indeed rare to encounter an item which convincingly displays the characteristics of Dunmore yet lacks such a mark. However, the incidence of genuine unmarked Dunmore may be higher than is commonly imagined. An indication of this comes from a catalogue of the collections held in the Smith Institute (now Art Gallery & Museum) in Stirling. In the 1934 edition, within the listings of their holdings of pottery, there is a section headed "Dunmore Ware". Twelve items are given brief descriptions, as follows (my comments appear within square brackets):

50	Tea tray, marked "Dunmore" [presumably mark 1 in my list, which follows].
51-52	Two fruit plates, marked "Peter Gardener, Dunmore Pottery" [a different misspelling of his surname from normal; presumably mark 3 in my list].
53-59	Child's tea service, seven pieces, stamped "Dunmore" [presumably mark1 again].
60	Small jar. [The lack of any mention of a mark, when this has been noted for the previous items, suggests that it was not marked.]
61	Tall jar with four ornaments of rope design, a piece of fine shape and colour, not stamped, but the donor was sole agent for Stirling until the pottery stopped work, and it was a stock piece. R. Adam & Son, Stirling. [The suspicion raised by the previous entry is here confirmed by the phrase "not stamped", yet the compiler of the catalogue has gone to some pains to verify that the item in question is a genuine Dunmore product.]

This catalogue entry means that some of the output of Dunmore Pottery lacked any form of maker's mark, though the evidence provided by extant pieces suggests that the proportion was very small. Why this should have happened at all is unclear. In the case of miniatures, there may simply have been insufficient room to apply the mark in a satisfactory fashion, but the tall jar (catalogue no. 61, accession no. 2314) is clearly an outstanding item, notwithstanding it being referred to as a "stock piece", and one which, it must be imagined, Peter Gardner would have been proud to have produced. It should be noted that all the items of Dunmore pottery illustrated in this booklet bear impressed marks, the only exception being the little advertising bowl (see Figure 17) which carries the identification "Dunmore Pottery" as part of its moulded inscription. Because of the importance bestowed upon Dunmore marks in the Proclamation, it might be a worthwhile exercise to tabulate them here. They are illustrated overleaf as per their actual size.

Dunmore Maker's Marks

Pre Peter Gardner

Because of the very ordinary nature of the goods made at Dunmore before Peter Gardner began to weave his magic, marking would not normally have been a consideration, and it was only when an exceptional item was produced that a mark would have been applied. An example of this may be seen on a splendid saut bucket (salt jar) dated 1846 bearing extensive modelled and incised decoration,[48] the execution of which would have required much time and effort, thus justifying such special treatment. In this case, the mark (see Figure 20) is treated as part of the decoration.

Figure 20

Peter Gardner's marks

A number of different marks were applied to Dunmore goods during the period of Peter Gardner by means of metal die-stamps.

No.1: the single word DUNMORE.
This is by far the commonest of the marks used by Peter Gardner (see Figure 21). Sometimes the impression is given that this did not come from a cast die, but from a stamp composed of individual characters from a letterpress, resulting in a slightly uneven line (see Figure 22).

Figure 21

Figure 22

No.1a: If the above speculation is correct, it would account for a variation where (i) the E is missing, giving DUNMOR – uncommon though not exactly rare. The defect was duly spotted, and the immediate response was to correct the error by hand by (ii) incising the terminal E into the clay after the defective stamp had been applied. A more effective solution was to (iii) replace the missing E, which at least corrected the spelling, but created a new problem, the point-size of the letterpress character sometimes being too large! (see Figure 23).

Figure 23

No.2: the phrase DUNMORE POTTERY, maintaining the same style of lettering; uncommon (see Figure 24).

Figure 24

No.3: two concentric circles containing PETER GARDNER between them, the names separated between the first letter of the forename and the final letter of the surname by a device, similar to a Maltese cross, with DUNMORE POTTERY in the central area, the words forming two arcs with the downturned arc above and the upturned arc below (see Figure 25 and back cover). This mark would seem to indicate that Peter Gardner, as the man largely or even wholly responsible for the unusual shapes and spectacular glazes of Dunmore products, in terms of both concept and execution, was keen to have this recognised by those who purchased and owned his wonderful creations. In this mark, which is quite common, his own name dominates that of his Pottery. (The Maltese cross separating device has been used to signify the location of Dunmore Pottery on the maps at the start of this booklet; see Figures 1 and 2.)

Figure 25

Post Peter Gardner

Another common mark is the single word DUNMORE but in *sans serif* lettering (see Figure 26). This was certainly used after Peter Gardner's time, though perhaps not exclusively so. The products on which it appears, while of competent manufacture, usually seem to lack the essential characteristics associated with Gardner's work. Some dated items are known, and these are post-1902, *i.e.* after Peter Gardner's death. Another mark from this period is the double-arced DUNMORE / POTTERY as if taken from the central portion of the Peter Gardner mark (No. 3 above); sometimes the single word DUNMORE is used. Again, pieces bearing such marks look as if they belong to the post-Gardner period.

Figure 26

(It should be said here that the above assessment, and indeed the whole table of Dunmore marks, is based upon examining hundreds of Dunmore items over several decades. That, of course, does not provide a guarantee of completeness or total accuracy, and it may be that the exhibition at Stirling Museum which this booklet accompanies will bring to light examples which will cause this section to be reappraised.)

Royal and noble patronage

The Proclamation terminates with a statement indicating that Dunmore Pottery had received attention and patronage from the very top levels of the society, including nobility and even royalty:

> "A great many of the Patterns have been furnished by the Earl and Countess and Dowager Countess of Dunmore, and have secured the distinguished patronage of Her Most Gracious Majesty the Queen, and very many of the Nobility".

It should be remembered that Peter Gardner, like his father and grandfather, did not own Dunmore Pottery, but ran it as a tenant of the Earl of Dunmore on whose estate it was situated. Happily for Gardner, he had a landlord who was sympathetic to his endeavours, and one factor in the success achieved by Dunmore products was surely the encouragement given by the Earl concerning the making and promotion of the wares. He even allowed his name to be used for promotional purposes in a way which amounted to commercial exploitation; advertisements for Dunmore pottery appeared below the heading "Under the Patronage of the Earl of Dunmore" (see Figure 9). The man in question was Charles Adolphus Murray (1841-1907), Viscount Fincastle, and Baron Murray of Blair, Moulin, and Tillemot, in the peerage of Scotland (created 1686); and Baron Dunmore, in that of the United Kingdom (created 1831).[49] His two seats were Dunmore Park in Stirlingshire, and Ruadhal on the island of Harris. Charles Murray (see Figure 27) succeeded as the 7th Earl of Dunmore in 1845. In addition to his array of noble titles, the Earl of Dunmore was a man of considerable importance. He was Lord Lieutenant of the County of Stirling from 1875 to 1885, and a Lord in Waiting to Queen Victoria between 1874 and 1880. (The position of Lord in Waiting was considerably more important than the female equivalent, a position which had been held by his mother, necessary though that was; he had to attend ceremonial and state functions, to represent the monarch in her absence at official events, and to welcome important visitors on behalf of the Queen.)

Being so intimately connected with the working life of the sovereign for a period of six years was not the only royal liaison enjoyed by the Earl of Dunmore, for he was also on very friendly terms with the Prince of Wales (later King Edward VII). Their friendship went back a long way. In the family archive there is a letter written on paper bearing the embossed royal arms and "Osborne" (a favourite residence of Queen Victoria, on the Isle of Wight), addressed to the future Earl of Dunmore when he was still a boy of 12, and sent to Whitmarsh Rectory near Leamington (or, to give it its full name, Royal Leamington Spa, in Warwickshire). It is in the hand of and signed by "Albert Edward" (the Prince of Wales), and dated 29th November 1853, when he also was aged just 12. It starts "My dear Dunmore" and thanks him for some service rendered, then adds "I am glad you have not forgotten the days you spent with me a Buckingham Palace, and I hope we shall be able to play there together again".[50] The Prince and the Princess of Wales (later Queen Alexandra) attended the Earl's wedding at Holkham in Norfolk in 1866. The Prince was a sponsor (god-parent) to the Earl's eldest son, Alexander, and attended his baptism at the Chapel Royal in St James's Palace, London, in 1871. (The Queen herself was a sponsor to the Earl's fourth daughter, Victoria, who was born in 1877.) There were no particular criteria which qualified members of the peerage to have an infant sponsored by royalty, although it was certainly an honour. It is disappointing that in spite of the Earl's connections with the Royal Court, and with the Prince of Wales in particular, there are very few published references to him, and he is barely mentioned in the official biography of King Edward VII by Sir Sidney Lee. The single passing reference to the Earl of Dunmore is contained in a comment made by the Marquis of Lincolnshire when visiting Sandringham shortly after the accession of Edward VII in 1901. "I could hardly realise that the Prince of Wales was King. He seemed so entirely himself, and with all the old surroundings it seemed as if the old days were back again. When the Queen retired we all went into the smoking-room, which was the same as ever…and the whole thing brought back memories of…[he names nine members of Edward's social circle, including:] Charlie Dunmore".[51] Presumably this refers to Charles Adolphus Murray, the Earl of Dunmore. Such familiarity demonstrates the very pally nature of the relationship which existed between the members of this elevated cadre.

Figure 27

The Earl of Dunmore's friendship with the Prince of Wales caused the future king to visit Dunmore Park on a number of occasions, for it was a friendship which was to endure. In the autumn of 1870, for instance, Prince Edward spent several days in Stirlingshire, his main activity being shooting on the Polmaise and Touchadam estates, though it is reported that on the Sunday he drove to Dunmore Park to visit the Earl of Dunmore. (This being a few years before the launch of the 'new Dunmore', it is unlikely that the Pottery would have featured in his itinerary.) Certainly Prince Edward visited Dunmore on more than one occasion, and it has even been rumoured that his private visits became so regular that the cost of laying on lavish hospitality contributed to the financial difficulties which overtook the Earl of Dunmore. In his standard work *Scottish Pottery* of 1923, Arnold Fleming dates one visit to "about the year 1871",[52] but he is notoriously shaky regarding dates; even so, some later writers give this as the precise year. In addition, other dates are sometimes cited.[53] Paradoxically, a non-event of 1873 may actually have played a significant part in the story. Press reports show that by April of that year, excitement was mounting in Stirlingshire regarding the forthcoming visit of the Prince of Wales, but in June it all fell through because of the visit to Britain of Russian royalty (being the Princess of Wales' close family). The Earl of Dunmore informed the Provost of Stirling "with extreme regret" of the cancellation, and a local newspaper, which reprinted that letter, commented on the "considerable disappointment" felt in Stirling at the news. It is possible that among those who experienced this emotion was Peter Gardner. It transpires that the Prince's stay in Stirling that autumn was to have included a visit to the Highland and Agricultural Society's annual show. Given the Earl of Dunmore's reputation in cattle-breeding circles and his high social standing, he might well have been in a position of influence with the Society's hierarchy which would have enabled him to assist Peter Gardner in displaying the 'new Dunmore' ware at the Show – if it had been ready at that time. If this suggestion is regarded as a realistic possibility, it could be that the absence of this royal patron of Dunmore products caused such a postponement, in which case the 'new Dunmore' might have been kept under wraps for a year, to be unveiled at the next Highland Show, that of 1874 in the somewhat distant location of Inverness. The possibility therefore exists that the fame achieved by Dunmore ware was delayed for a year because of the visit of the Russian in-laws of the future king.

One proposed visit which did take place can be verified thanks to a newspaper article which appeared in 1876. Most of the report is taken up with an account of the Prince's arrival at Stirling railway station and his procession through the town. As it was not a formal visit, he was dressed casually: "His Royal Highness looked in good health, and wore a grey Ulster and a brown hat, a dress in which – were it not that his cartes have rendered his features familiar to everybody – he might without further disguise play the part of the 'Gude Man of Ballengeich' [a reference to the habit of King James V of wandering incognito – or so he imagined – among his subjects, dressed in plain clothing]".[54] The Prince of Wales was welcomed immediately on arrival by the Earl of Dunmore, and by a reception committee headed by the Provost of Stirling. He was then driven by the Earl to Dunmore Park in a carriage and four, with two postillions and an outrider. The reporter described the visit as "being of a private and friendly nature, [and so] only a few guests were present", adding: "One of the principal attractions to the Prince at Dunmore was, we are told, an inspection of the magnificent herd of shorthorns which the noble Earl owns".

Another possible reason for the visit also concerned livestock and could have involved Peter Gardner. Edward was well-known for his fondness of horse racing. Indeed, his biographer Sir Sidney Lee remarked: "The King's principal recreation was racing, a sport of which he never grew tired…..to the end, the King's horses offered him deep gratification".[55] This would have provided a common bond with the master potter of Dunmore, of whom Arnold Fleming has recorded: "Peter Gardner had also sporting proclivities, and in his day was well known throughout Scotland as a trainer and breeder of Arab steeds".[56] (There were certainly horses in the immediate vicinity a little later; the Valuation Rolls for 1894 show that the grass park known as Pottery Field was leased to Alexander Scott, horse owner.) The newspaper report finishes with the information that the visit lasted from Saturday afternoon until Monday morning, when the Earl drove the Prince to Airth Road railway station; there is not a word about Peter Gardner and his pots, nor even his steeds.

It might be hoped that the royal diaries could provide some detail of the visit which would throw a little light on the activities of the Pottery at this time. Alas, there is no narrative, the brief entries being restricted to engagements.[57] Those for the relevant period read as follows:
> 9 September
> Leave Abergeldie 10 am. [Abergeldie Castle on the Balmoral Estates was the Prince of Wales' residence when in Scotland.] Arrive at Stirling 5.30. Received by Ld. Dunmore

& drive to Dunmore [Park]. Dinner – Lord Dunmore, Lord Elphinstone, Ladies Mary and Mildred Coke, Hon. H. & Lady Margaret Strutt, Capt. Hon. O. Montague, Mr Berwick.

10 September

Mr F. Knollys arrives. Morning service 11. At Dunmore. Visit Farms & Herd of Shorthorns. Dinner as 9 September.

11 September

Leave Dunmore 8.45.

The accuracy of the newspaper report is thus verified, though not necessarily its completeness, although if the Prince of Wales had visited Peter Gardner at his workplace, it might be expected that the occasion would have been noted in the royal diary, however briefly. Nevertheless, the certain knowledge that the Prince of Wales did visit Dunmore, more than once, lends a degree of authenticity to the story given in Arnold Fleming's book that he also took in the Pottery: "While staying with the Earl and Countess, King Edward VII, then Prince of Wales, paid a visit to the pottery, and thus gave it a further advertisement, and caused 'Dunmore Ware' to become fashionable in Royal and Society circles, in every style and in all manner of shapes, sizes and colours".[58] This account led a modern journalist, John Jenkinson, to eulogise: "Dunmore Pottery was so highly esteemed that even the curiosity of the Prince of Wales was aroused to such a height that he made a pilgrimage to observe the potter at work".[59] This is a somewhat colourful interpretation of the meagre evidence available, but it may well be true. It is also possible that Peter Gardner made a souvenir of the event, for one of his many notable products is a jug in the shape of a dragon, with its head tilted backwards, its mouth forming the aperture, the whole covered with a rich red glaze (see Figure C22). It was a colour which impressed Fleming, who commented on it (though not specifically on this jug) thus: "The crimson glaze was very rich, and had a soft deep luscious tint".[60] What more appropriate a way to commemorate a visit by the Prince of Wales than the production of a red dragon? (It should be noted, though, that some of these jugs bear a green glaze.) It has been said that in order to do justice to his visit to the works, the Prince spent the night in Dunmore Pottery House, an elegant villa in which Peter Gardner lived with his sisters and a number of pottery workers (see Figure 28). It has the appearance of being late Georgian or early Victorian, and might well have been built by his father, whose property transactions indicate that he probably had sufficient funds at his disposal. If Edward was resident here, for however brief a period of time, it might account for the creation of the special room located in the single-storey east wing of the house, measuring 19½ feet by 14½ feet. It perhaps functioned as the display room for the pottery being produced, and was certainly a display feature in its own right. Fleming recorded this picture of it: "I remember him [Peter Gardner] showing me a room in his house, the walls, floor and ceiling of which were entirely composed of his coloured glazed pottery".[61] Alas, he gives no further details of this amazing form of decoration, though he does offer a somewhat nervous aside: "Although a remarkable display of craftsmanship, I must confess that sitting in this room I was in constant dread lest some heavy portion of the ceiling might crack and fall down on my head". For the true devotee of Dunmore pottery, what a way to go!

The description of this room sounds as if it was indeed fit for a prince, so Edward might well have spent the night in it. Supporting the possibility is the story (citied by Robin Hill) that a

Figure 28

special royal lavatory was constructed, each diamond-shaped floor tile being embellished with the Prince of Wales' feathers.[62] When the Royal Commission on the Ancient and Historical Monuments of Scotland surveyed the site in 1976, they recounted that "There was a decoratively tiled lavatory in an outbuilding south-east of the house"[63] (at a distance of 15 paces, according to the RCAHMS record sheets). They published a drawing of a wall urinal, including vertical and horizontal sections;[64] the actual object (see Figure C25) is now in Huntly House Museum, Edinburgh. They also have on record a photograph of a portion of the lavatory floor which was found in 1963,[65] showing rhombic tiles arranged in alternating rows according to the decoration they bore – either unpatterned mottled glazing, or a device which may be a simplified version of either a *fleur-de-lys* (iris) or the Prince of Wales' feathers. These latter tiles carry the design apparently incised in outline and filled in with glaze; two of them are also preserved in Huntly House (see Figures C26 and C27), having been presented at that time by the Museum's Superintendent, George Young. Nonetheless, it must be admitted that the evidence for this room being created to serve as the Prince of Wales' quarters, if only for a brief period, is not strong and is somewhat equivocal. If it was so, then it was certainly added to later, for the ceiling centre-piece, in the shape of a large star (16½ inches in diameter), was found to bear the incised inscription "Dunmore Pottery 1887" in a sweeping copperplate hand (see Figure 29) on its reverse side – and consequently invisible as long as it remained in position! The mark illustrated here is much reduced; the word 'Pottery' is actually 11 inches in width. A possible pointer is the royal coat of arms appearing in relief on a tile above the fire-place (see Figure C32); but that could also be explained by Queen Victoria's purchase of items of Dunmore pottery while in

Edinburgh in 1886, an occasion which might even have provided the inspiration for the construction of this unique room.

The tragedy is that this room was not preserved for posterity, for it must have been truly magnificent. Arnold Fleming does not give a date for his visit, but he retired from his business as proprietor of the Britannia Pottery in Glasgow in 1920, and his book on the history of Scottish Pottery was published in 1923, so it might have been between those dates, and was certainly no later than the second of them. The Pottery had ceased functioning by then, and over the succeeding decades the room gradually deteriorated. By the mid 1960s, it was seen by one visitor, Oonagh Morrison, as "rapidly crumbling into disrepair", though she could still appreciate it as "a poignantly evocative reminder of Dunmore's erstwhile fame". Her overall impression was that "it is all rather a hotch-potch stylistically, but it captures the extravagant spirit of the Victorian age".[66] A similar opinion was expressed by an inspector with the Royal Commission on the Ancient and Historical Monuments of Scotland, Geoffrey Hay: "The variety and proliferation of tiles concedes more to the display of the potter's art than to any attempt at a rational décor".[67] Morrison also noted, significantly, that a portrait of the Prince of Wales hung above the mantelpiece (though she wrongly identified the armorial tile mentioned above as displaying the Dunmore coat of arms). She explained Edward's presence in a later article: "The portrait remains to commemorate the Prince's patronage";[68] but there is no mention of him actually staying in that room.

Eventually, with the workings of the Pottery a distant memory and the property having changed hands on several occasions, the special room was dismantled in 1975/6. I was fortunate enough to see it, albeit in a semi-desolate state, yet still emitting strong echoes of its glorious past. Neither my memory of that day, nor my camera loaded with black and white film, can do it justice now, but before the room was dismantled completely, it was visited by inspectors from the Royal Commission on the Ancient and Historical Monuments of Scotland, and a photographic record made of areas of tiling in situ, and groups detached of tiles laid out in order, both in black and white and in colour. Of particular interest are shots of the fireplace, fire surround, and mirror surround above, with the spectacular tile arrangement still intact. In addition, Ken McKay, an industrial physicist with a keen interest in old industrial buildings and processes, had visited the house in November 1972 and took a number of colour photographs. A selection are illustrated here (Figures C30, C31, and C32), and they provide a vivid impression of how the room must have looked in its erstwhile splendour. We may yet see something of that

Figure 29

splendour restored, for although the dismantled tiles were put on the market, negotiations enabled them to be purchased, in several lots, by Edinburgh City Museums, with the intention of someday recreating that famous room.

The collection consists of well over 500 tiles.[69] There are some 337 square tiles, 56 rectangular ones, and 87 of other shapes, such as stellate, rhombic, and circular. There are also quite a number of tiles made as fittings, such as sections of chamfered cornice, and others made to perform specific functions, such as finger-plates. A number of the tiles have screw-holes to aid fixing, and indeed some are still attached to fitments taken from the room – a cast-iron fire-place and mantelpiece, and a large glazed door. It is possible that these were displayed at the Glasgow International Exhibition of 1888, as described in a newspaper report: "A mantelpiece mirror with frame in tile medallions, consisting of figures drawn with exceeding taste, is placed predominantly at the back of the stand. Underneath there is the frame of a new style of grate with figured pottery frieze of rare turquoise blue colour".[70] A visitor to the unique room installed in Dunmore Pottery House would hardly have needed reminding where they were, yet there are seven ceramic letters of the alphabet, each 7 inches high, which, arranged in what must be assumed is the correct order, spell DUNMORE (*sans serif* style). They have been given an ochre glaze, and each has screw-holes, thus: 3-3-4-4-2-4-4. Perhaps they were used by Peter Gardner on his display stand when he participated in prestigious exhibitions.

Many of the square tiles are moulded with motifs in high relief, usually being decorated in a single-colour glaze, with only the most salient features being given a splash of another colour (see Figure C30). The favourite themes are fruit (apples, plums, pears, and strawberries) and animals (rabbits, grouse, ducks, and hens). Many other square tiles, while devoid of any moulded design, carry a spectacular array of multi-coloured glazes, applied in spatter fashion (also Figure C30). Pre-dating San Francisco psychedelia by something like 80 years, it is hard to imagine them fitting into a Victorian domestic colour scheme, and they might have been produced for display purposes only, so that Peter Gardner could show potential clients the dramatic range of colours which he was capable of producing. By contrast, others of a deep reddish brown mimic mahogany (again Figure 30). The rectangular tiles, both horizontal and vertical, exhibit some most intriguing designs. There is one showing a group of naked children with a goat; some of them are holding it steady, while one attempts to climb on its back as another one tumbles off. One of the children is holding a mask in front of his face, depicting a man with a long beard and large nose. On another tile, a girl is shown milking a sheep with a lamb in close attendance, the milk being directed into a rather elegant pedestalled bowl, a larger version of which stands behind her adjacent to a wooden coggie, this being a more expected receptacle. Most unusually, large areas of the background to this scene are left blank. By way of total contrast, there are Bacchanalian scenes crowded with lively figures and a variety of bizarre accoutrements (again Figure C30). There are also some more conventional drinking scenes, each of three different designs showing a group of people sitting round a table, others standing, with lots of detail regarding furnishings and utensils, including pots. More fanciful is the design of an elegant lady attired only in jewellery – necklace, bracelets, ear-rings, and a tiara. A long, flowing cloth swirls gracefully, mostly behind her. On another, a figure reminiscent of a medieval knight stands defiantly, grasping a pennanted staff in his right hand while his left rests on the pommel of his sword, with his shield at his feet. Beneath him there is an owl, more heraldic than natural; it also appears many times on its own on smaller tiles. In classical mould are two tiles with profile heads in shallow relief, captioned 'Agrippa' and 'Paris' respectively. Another design shows two winged cherubs in flight, holding an ornate Grecian-style urn between them. There is also an unusual circular tile depicting a Chinese or possibly Japanese warrior in traditional attire holding aloft a large bronze bowl.

A number of these designs are repeated several times, and may be glazed in different colours; ochre, brown, green, and turquoise are the most common. The turquoise glaze is used a great deal, which is perhaps surprising considering that the *Visit* booklet describes it as "a rare and expensive colour to produce". It may therefore be taken as confirmation that this room was indeed very special. It certainly is an appealing colour (see Figure C23), though its effectiveness is sometimes diminished when the glaze consistency is too thick (not an uncommon fault), in which case it tends to clog up the finer features of the moulded design. Curiously, the tiles showing the drinking scenes were left unglazed in fawn bisque.

Though bereft of its spectacular room, Dunmore Pottery House lived on, and even enjoyed something of a resurgence in its later days. It was renovated, and run as a hotel by Airth man Bill Mitchell in the early 1980s. He had various items of Dunmore pottery on display, and even reproduced an old photograph of the house and nearby kiln on the place-mats in his restaurant! (see Figure 28). In the later 1980s, it was taken over by Sandy Mackie, who ran it as the Dunmore Pottery Inn (see Figure 30). Sadly, neither of these ventures achieved long-term success, and the house fell vacant once more. Right at the end of the 20th century, the land was acquired by a developer for housing. Dunmore Pottery House was used for a period as the site office, and then,

Figure 30

despite pleas that it should be saved as a building of historical significance, it was demolished in 2002 – just a matter of weeks after the centenary of the death of Peter Gardner, which was a cruelly inappropriate way to commemorate that occasion.

In its heyday, Dunmore Pottery had certainly received the support of the Earl of Dunmore, as already discussed, but the booklet *A Visit to Dunmore Pottery* refers to both the Earl and the Countess. This lady was Gertrude Coke, daughter of the Earl of Leicester, who married the 7th Earl of Dunmore in 1866. It is she who is generally credited as assuming a very active part in pottery production at Dunmore. Arnold Fleming states: "From the beginning, the Countess of Dunmore took a deep practical interest in this young potter's operations, supplying him not merely with inspiration and encouragement, but also with designs, even taking an active part in the business, and supervising the production of the wares….Many of the rustic ornaments and elegant vases, some of which I illustrate (Plate XLVII), were from designs furnished by the

Countess herself ". [71] Fleming's photograph is reproduced here (see Figure 31), and some of those pieces (the first two and the last one) are shown in the colour section (see Figures C13, C17, and C16). On the subject of rustic wares, a degree of caution, even scepticism, is necessary when considering Fleming's claim that "their rustic tea-sets were also unique in design and execution", as this writer has not encountered any Dunmore examples of this genre which come up to the rustic qualities of the likes of Bailey of Alloa and Belfield of Prestonpans, or even Murray of the Caledonian Pottery in Glasgow – and these factories registered their designs (in 1872/3, 1876, and 1877 respectively), which is something that Peter Gardner never did. It also seems a little curious that Fleming should describe Peter Gardner as a "young potter" at this time, as he was already forty years of age when the first of the 'new Dunmore' wares were produced.

It should be noted, however, that the *Visit* booklet names *three* members of the Dunmore family who lent their assistance to Peter Gardner's Pottery, the third being the Dowager Countess of Dunmore, and it is this lady whom family tradition asserts should receive most of the credit for bolstering the activities of the Pottery.[72] Such a contention receives affirmation from an article published in the *Art Journal* in 1880, which attributes the success which Dunmore ware had achieved by then "chiefly to the good taste of the Dowager Countess of Dunmore, who has devoted herself to the encouragement and improvement of this local industry".[73] This lady was Catherine Herbert, daughter of the Earl of Pembroke and grand-daughter of the Russian Ambassador to Great Britain, who married Alexander Edward Murray, 6th Earl of Dunmore, in 1836, just six weeks before he succeeded to the title. When he died in 1845, she became Dowager Countess, though she would not have been commonly known by that title until the 7th Earl got married, which he did in 1866, his wife thereby becoming the new Countess of Dunmore. Lady Catherine was certainly active in the local community, doing good works. In 1854, for instance, she was joint patroness with the Duchess of Montrose of a 'Bazaar of Fancy Work' which was held for the benefit of the Ragged and Industrial School run by Stirling Town Council.[74]

Figure 31

Fancy Frogs

Figure C1

Figure C2

Figure C3

*The five single pots shown in the **Visit** booklet*

Figure C4

Figure C5

Figure C6

Figure C7

Figure C8

Three types of ware mentioned in the *Visit* booklet

Figure C9

Figure C10

Figure C11

Figure C12

Eight notable items of Dunmore ware

Figure C13

Figure C14

Figure C15

Figure C16

Figure C17

Figure C18

Figure C19

Figure C20

Some other special Dunmore items

Figure C21

Figure C22

Figure C23

Figure C24

From the Dunmore Pottery House lavatory

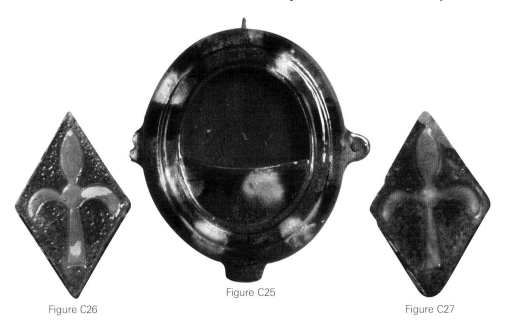

Figure C26

Figure C25

Figure C27

Figure C28

Figure C29

The tiled room in Dunmore Pottery House

Figure C30

Figure C31

Figure C32

Dunmore Pottery main kiln

Figure C33

In the following year, 1855, Lady Catherine headed the list of patronesses of a similar enterprise in aid of the Episcopal School in Stirling.[75] It was closer to home, however, that both elements of that latter project, education and Episcopalian worship, felt the benefit of her endeavours. She was the prime mover in the erection of St Andrew's Chapel on the Dunmore estate in 1850, dedicated to the memory of her late husband, for the benefit of local people of that religious persuasion (a beautifully fitted-up little building, the recent demolition of which is much regretted). Even though Airth had two schools (the Parish School and the Adventure School), she was the sponsor of what was called the Dowager Countess of Dunmore's School. The Dunmore estate itself benefited directly from her diligent attention to its needs – and perhaps her own needs too, as exemplified by the redevelopment of the hamlet of Dunmore.

A local newspaper of 1856 explains: "Within the last few years, this small hamlet has been greatly transformed. That truly excellent lady, the Countess of Dunmore, has done much to adorn and beautify the village, as well as add to the comfort of a great many of its residents. From time to time, the old houses have been disappearing, and cottages of the most beautiful architecture, in conformance with the Elizabethan style, built in their room".[76] This non-Scottish style was reportedly chosen because of Lady Catherine's desire to see buildings which reflected the architecture of her homeland. Dunmore is described in the Ordnance Survey Name Book of 1862 as "A clean and compact little village…It has recently undergone extensive improvements, by most of the old houses being taken down and replaced with neat cottages. It contains a population of nearly 200". The result is an undeniably charming little enclave, a noteworthy feature of which is the doorway to the old blacksmith's premises which takes the form of a huge inverted horseshoe, in masonry. In the centre of the green is a font under a columned canopy, made of cast iron (in London, despite the proximity of the renowned Carron Iron Works!), with a panel bearing the inscription: "The School and Village of Dunmore, together with this well, built by Catherine Herbert, Countess of Dunmore, were completed A.D. 1879". The newspaper report also implies that her influence was to be seen in the improvements taking place over the entire estate, "there being scarcely a steading but what has either undergone or is undergoing repairs, getting additional offices and outhouses built, and several of them have obtained new dwelling-houses, most elegant in structure, combining everything requisite for health and comfort, being large, airy, and convenient, and, when taken along with the offices, &c., may well be looked upon as models of what steadings ought to be, when taking into consideration the advanced state of modern farming."

There is no doubting that the Countess played a major role in the administration of the Dunmore estate, including Dunmore Pottery. In 1855, the Valuation Rolls (in their first year of operation) give the proprietor of the Pottery as "the Countess of Dunmore, Tutor to the Earl of Dunmore, per John Lockhart, Factor". A tutor (in this context, meaning guardian) was necessary because the Earl was still a minor. (As indicated two years later, Lockhart had his work-base at Park Terrace in Stirling, though his home was in the combined factor's house and parsonage on the estate. His working relationship with Peter Gardner has not so far been determined.) It was only in 1884, two years before her death, that the Countess handed over the running of the estate to trustees. She was generally involved in arts and crafts in the community, and took a particular interest in the manufactures which were being practised on both of the principal Dunmore family estates, doing much the same for tweed production on Harris as she did for pottery production at Dunmore.[77] She gave birth to the last of her four children in 1845, just four days after becoming a widow.

Lady Catherine's obituary in the local newspaper described her as "a lady universally respected and esteemed", adding that "some idea of the high esteem in which the noble lady was held could be gathered from the array of magnificent wreaths and crosses sent to adorn the grave. One from her Majesty the Queen, who also sent a letter and a telegram of sympathy, bore the words 'A token of affectionate regard' [the Countess had been Lady of the Bedchamber to Queen Victoria]…During her long connection with the district, she never ceased to promote and encourage every institution which affected its welfare, spiritually, intellectually, and physically".[78] What a pity this sentence deals only in generalities, without making a specific reference to her interest in the Pottery.

An elegant portrait of Lady Catherine Dunmore was painted in 1841, when she was aged 27, by which time she had held the title of Countess of Dunmore for five years. The artist was Robert Thorburn (1818-1885) who hailed from Dumfriesshire, and had studied at the Trustees' Academy in Edinburgh before moving to London. He specialised in miniatures until the advent of photography compelled him to change to large-scale portraiture. In 1845, he painted Queen Victoria, Prince Albert, and two of their children, his work being renowned for the grace and dignity which he imparted to his subjects. His rendition of Lady Catherine Dunmore was etched by J. Jenkins II, and reproduced by William and Edward Finden in their *Portraits of the Female Aristocracy of the Court of Queen Victoria* in 1849 (see frontispiece to this booklet). Rather a fine portrait sketch was made of Lady Catherine Dunmore in 1849, when she was aged 35. The artist was James Rannie Swinton (1816-1868) who came from the Borders and had also trained at the Trustees' Academy in Edinburgh. He specialised in portraits, mostly of society and aristocratic figures, painting in oil and also drawing in crayon. He lived in London (at 1 St. George's Road, Eccleston Square, in 1849) and in Rome, and became wealthy from the proceeds of his portraiture. His rendition of Lady Catherine suggests a person of charm and sensitivity. The portrait was drawn on stone and produced as a lithograph (see Figure 32) by Richard J. Lane (1800-1872), whose studio at that time was at 12 Queen's Row, Gloucester Gate, London. He was elected Associate of the Royal Academy of Arts in 1827, and produced a number of portraits of members of the Royal Family. Although he exhibited several of his lithographs of Swinton portraits featuring society ladies at the Royal Academy between 1849 and 1855, that of Lady Catherine Dunmore would not seem to have been among them. The portrait illustrated here hangs in the home of the current Countess of Dunmore, and another print may be seen in the New Club premises in Edinburgh. She has no local memorial (unless the planned hamlet of Dunmore is regarded in this light), nor can her grave be identified in the family burial ground beside Elphinstone Tower on the estate, which is badly overgrown and in a poor state of preservation, though her husband, son, and daughter-in-law are all commemorated there with impressive tombstones. However, she may have what is ultimately a more fitting testimonial to her involvement with Dunmore Pottery – a rather special piece which was named after her (see note on the booklet Frontispiece, section II).

Figure 32

It is worth remembering that the situation at Dunmore was not unique among the potteries in the East of Scotland. Just across the River Forth, the Alloa Pottery was also located on land belonging to a member of the nobility, a circumstance which the Pottery used to its advantage. Some products, as well as carrying the usual maker's mark W. & J.A. BAILEY / ALLOA, have an additional impressed mark: MANUFACTURED ON THE ESTATE OF / THE EARL OF MAR & KELLIE. Presumably it was thought that promoting this aristocratic link would be of commercial benefit. A degree of aristocratic patronage comparable to the Dunmore situation may be detected at little further away, at Kirkcaldy, regarding the famous Wemyss Ware produced by Robert Heron & Son in the Fife Pottery at Gallatown. In the book on *Wemyss Ware* by Peter Davis and Robert Rankine, the connection is clearly stated: "The name for Wemyss Ware seems to have been taken from the Wemyss family of neighbouring Wemyss Castle, who continued to take a keen amateur interest in its development, just as the Countess of Dunmore had done in the development of Dunmore Ware...Two popular Wemyss vases have particularly close associations with members of the family from Wemyss Castle. The Lady Eva vase with its wide undulating rim was named after Lady Eva Wemyss. The Grosvenor vase, which has a characteristic piecrust rim, was named after Lady Henry Grosvenor, who was Miss Dora Mina Wemyss before marriage. Her contribution to the success of the new ware was to introduce Wemyss to her circle of influential friends, particularly in fashionable London. Robert Heron named the Grosvenor vase after her as a compliment".[79] This would seem to provide a direct parallel with the Lady Dunmore bowl.

The death of the Dowager Countess of Dunmore at Carberry Tower near Musselburgh in 1886 was no doubt sorely felt at the Pottery, and it is also a matter of sadness that she did not live quite long enough to enjoy the successes which Dunmore products met with at the Edinburgh International Exhibition. There is an anachronism in the booklet here, for it refers to an event which occurred at that Exhibition (which opened on 6th May 1886) in the past tense, yet the Dowager Countess had died earlier that year on 12th February, and therefore should have been referred to as the 'late Dowager Countess'. This would suggest that the preface to the booklet (what I have termed the Proclamation) was composed some time in advance of the writing of the main body of text describing *A Visit to Dunmore Pottery*, and that it had been produced as a form of publicity by Peter Gardner at some point prior to the visit of the reporter.

Be that as it may, the interest and support of three members of the Dunmore family must have been of significant benefit to Peter Gardner in his endeavours. Eventually, however, their involvement faded as the ownership of the Dunmore estate entered an uncertain period. It is clear that all was not well, and in 1892, Edinburgh solicitors Dundas & Wilson published *Particulars of the Magnificent Residential Estate of Dunmore* (the publication is not actually dated, but references to crops, land values, etc., all apply to the year 1892). Regrettably, the Pottery is not mentioned in the text describing the various elements of the estate, but it is listed in an appendix giving the rental values of all the properties which were tenanted out. It appears under the heading 'Farms', covering almost 22 acres, with Peter Gardner as tenant. At the end of the volume there is a lithographed map, hand-tinted to show the different elements which comprised the Estate; the Pottery and its lands are indicated, but only as a single unit with little in the way of detail. A version of this map in the Smith Museum shows the area of the Pottery lands as having been bisected by the South Alloa branch railway line, with two approximately rectangular buildings shown just eastwards of the railway, corresponding with the Pottery's position on Ordnance Survey maps. This document was published on behalf of "the Trustees of the Rt. Hon. Charles Adolphus, Earl of Dunmore". Clearly, not just the management but the very ownership of the Estate was in a period of crisis. Burke's Peerage (apparently lagging a little behind the times) continued to list the Earl's seat as Dunmore Park in 1899, but not in 1900. By this time, Peter Gardner's involvement with pottery production was probably much reduced, as he was an elderly man in failing health. The break-up of the Dunmore Estate was not immediate, however, and the Pottery was to linger on well into the 20th century, with its final flicker perhaps coming in 1917. A sale catalogue was published in that year announcing that the Residential Estate of Dunmore of around 1,755 acres was to be auctioned by E. J. Castiglione, Sons & Scott, of Edinburgh, at the Golden Lion Hotel in Stirling on 20th September 1917, and the "Potter's Shop" was still recognisable as such at that time.[80]

For that purpose, the Estate was divided up into 45 lots. The first consisted of Dunmore Park mansion house and its policies; the next five all related to the Pottery. They are detailed below, their positions being given in relation to the Pottery buildings as designated on the accompanying map.

Lot 2: "Grass park known as West Potter Park" of 12.178 acres (annual rental value £17), immediately to the west. It was called "West Pottery Park" in the summary.

Lot 3: "Dunmore Pottery, comprising House containing Parlour, Kitchen, Scullery, and four Bedrooms; two Cottages, each with Kitchen and Bedroom; Stable, Barn, Kilns, Potter's Shop, etc." (rental £30). It was let to Thomas Harrison on a six year lease, though it operated only briefly, if at all. He had been a potter at Dunmore for at least 36 years, according to the Census Returns, and was 61 years old by this time (see Appendix A).

Lot 4: "Grass park known as Mid-Pottery Park" of 11.298 acres of "good grazing land" (rental £20), immediately to the north.

Lot 5: "Grazing land known as Pottery Field" of 24.455 acres of "rich pasture land" (rental £45 5s), immediately to the east.

Lot 6: "Two Cottages known as Holly Walk", each containing one room and kitchen (rental £6 2s.), immediately to the south of the previous lot. Let to James Downs. These cottages had previously been occupied by Pottery workers.

No unifying name is given, but one of great pertinence did exist. A transaction concerning the repayment of an improvement loan to the Scottish Drainage and Improvement Company in 1875 specifies a number of farms on the Dunmore Estate, including "Dunmore Pottery Farm".[81] It may be noted that the three grassy parks listed above with names tying them to the Pottery had a total annual rental value of £82 5s., as opposed to just £30 for the Pottery itself. Of course, it was close to closure at this point, and there is no mention of the condition of the works, which might have actually ceased to function by this time.

With the Earl of Dunmore losing control of the Dunmore estate at the end of the 19th century, followed soon after by the death of his talented tenant Peter Gardner, his interest in the Pottery thereafter is likely to have been minimal if at all. He died in London in 1907, though his wife lived on until 1943. The Earl's obituary in *The Times* recalled that "he was a great traveller, and his magnificent physique enabled him to penetrate regions full of hardship – Kashmir, Western Tibet, Chinese Tartary, and Russian Central Asia…his narrative of his experiences shows him to have been a man of no slight powers of observation and description".[82] There is a passing reference to Dunmore Park, but no mention of his interest in Dunmore Pottery.

A Visit to Dunmore Pottery.

Figure 33

The decorative feature at the top of the page and the title (Figure 33), and the huge initial letter of the text (Figure 34), are all copied from the original publication. The phrases which appear as quasi-headings or as captions, and the thumb-nail sketches, are inserted in their original positions. Beside each of the sketches of an individual piece is a photograph of the real item (though in one instance the comparison is questionable). They appear here in black and white, and they are also reproduced in full colour (see Figures C4-C8). For the sake of clarity and ease of legibility, the text is reproduced here to a larger size, and to aid comprehension of the sequence of operations, the text has been paragraphed to a greater extent than in the original, and sub-headings have been inserted, within square brackets, covering the introduction (colourful but not of great relevance), the various stages of production at Dunmore Pottery, and the conclusion. Numbers within square brackets refer to notes at the end of this section, which develop certain topics considered to be in need of explanation and/or worthy of extended comment.

[Introduction]

Figure 34

NE day last week I found myself at Larbert Station [1] on the way to visit the celebrated pottery at Dunmore, some four miles distant. It was the day before Falkirk Tryst, which is held on Stennis Muir [2], not far from the station; and the queer nondescript scene would have furnished subjects for the pencil of a Cruikshank [3] or a Doyle [4]. There were crowds of drovers and cattle-dealers, English and Scotch; Yorkshiremen, with their deep guttural dialect; Highlanders chattering voluble Gaelic; a seething crowd of plaided [5], mackintoshed [6], ulstered [7], booted humanity such as I never saw in my life before, each with a serviceable 'rung' [8] in his hand, and each, needless to mention, attended by a douce, business-like collie. I may safely say that the dog's faces were as characteristic as their masters', and that they seemed to understand their duties in dealing with recalcitrant cattle as well as the drover. Such herds of shaggy, long-horned Highland cattle, black and red and beaver-brown, such flocks of sheep, such odd groups on the moor RECALLING A SCENE OF PATRIARCHIAL ABUNDANCE, and, above all, such oceans of mud, in which a boat would not have seemed superfluous. The cattle gazed curiously at the cab, and seemed to ruminate as to the possibility of poking their long curved horns through the windows, the drovers rampaged and gesticulated, the dogs worked themselves into paroxysms of rage, and what between these distractions and talking over the humours of the fair, we were at Dunmore before we realised we had left Larbert.

Potteries are generally dull places planted in the midst of a waste, howling wilderness, and this one seemed no exception to the rule. If there *was* any scenery about Dunmore, it had retired within an impenetrable veil of mist, which added to the gloom of one of the most depressing, wet days I have every experienced. Even THE FAMOUS "WOODS OF DUNMORE" celebrated in song [9] looked an unattractive promenade for an ardent lover and his lass.

[A Tour of the Pottery]

At the pottery, however, all was bustle and life, and the various departments were in full swing. We were kindly received by the proprietor, Mr Gardner [10] , and in a very short time found ourselves under the guidance of an obliging and well-informed foreman [11] going over the work. The clay used here is mostly the native red clay of the district, supplemented by consignments from England [12] either for use along with the red Dunmore clay to form striped goods [13] or for the manufacture of different varieties of ware.

[Pugging]
Before using, the clay is carefully worked to extract any refuse, being mixed with water, passed through sieves, and finally boiled in a huge trough, by which process the water is evaporated. At this stage it is beautifully smooth, pliable, and elastic, and is then conveyed into a separate department to undergo the first stage in the process of emerging "a thing of beauty and a joy forever".

[Wedging]
In this department it is first kneaded very much as a baker manipulates dough, and is then ready for the potter and his wheel.

[Throwing]
It was very curious to look at his essentially simple and rude contrivance, and to think that for thousands of years it has remained practically unaltered [14]. Very much in its present form it is mentioned in the oldest of Books [15], it appears in

Egyptian paintings [16], and the mild Hindoo at the Colonial Exhibition [17] uses a similar contrivance to fashion his earthenware utensils. Simple as its construction may seem its achievements are marvellous. Seated by it the potter [18], who is here illustrated, takes up a lump of clay and throws it on the

Figure 35

Figure 36

revolving board. This board is driven by a wheel turned by a woman, and according to the article to be made she regulates the speed. Everything depends on this cunning adjustment, and the potter and the woman work in closest harmony. Under his busy and skilful fingers a teapot, a cream-jug, and a sugar basin successively took shape, smoothed inside and out, and presenting a very fair likeness to the original, as we know them. They looked

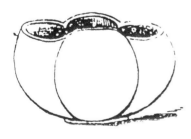

Figure 37

Figure 38

large, however, the reason of this being that the workman has to allow for the shrinking of the clay, which is at the rate of 1/8 in every inch. The tools used for the smoothing and shaping of these vessels were of the rudest. Pieces of iron, bits of slate, and a pair or two of callipers are all that are required, their use being regulated by the size of the article to be made. As the potter shaped and moulded the plastic clay into its various uses, making "one vessel to honour and another to dishonour", we envied him not a little his deftness, and retired greatly impressed by what we had seen.

Figure 39

Figure 40

[Turning and Burnishing]

The next metamorphosis of the clay was no less wonderful. We had seen the rude lumps fashioned into shapes which bore a close resemblance to the finished article, but had they been fired in that state they would have emerged mere caricatures of graceful and beautiful shapes. They had still to pass through

THE HANDS OF THE ARTIST,

whom we found standing before his lathe making the superfluous clay fly before his clever fingers. His tools, too, were of the simplest description – pieces of hoop iron variously pointed, but he had at least a hundred to choose from, each intended for a different article or a different part. As the shavings of clay fell away, lovely curves revealed themselves, sharp lines were traced, and straight ones accentuated; and then with a steel knife-like implement, he polished the dull clay until it had one uniform gloss. This worker, a tall, fine-looking, old man, whose speech yet retained traces of his distant Derbyshire home [19], was becomingly proud of his machine and the wonders it worked, and we went on more impressed than before by the marvels which rude machinery *plus* an artistic hand and eye may accomplish.

[Moulding and Fixing]

Following the career of the teapot which we have seen made thus far, the next stage is to give the finishing touches before firing, the body of the pot and the lid only being made by the potter and the turner. The spout, the handle, and the knob for the lid have all to be added, and their manipulation requires special care. For it is evident that they must not simply be stuck on, else they would soon part company with the main body in the firing, with disastrous consequences to themselves and the worker.

The handles, knobs, and spouts are made by a girl [20] and all lie in readiness for the various articles. She can make, she said, 288 spouts in a day. The spout is

Figure 41

MOULDED BY A FEW DEFT TOUCHES

in two parts, then put together and made to adhere. When it comes out of the mould it is trimmed, and then is ready for affixing.

[Fixing]
Our guide has this department under his special charge [21], and gave us an illustration of how a teapot is finished, the holes pricked in the side to keep back the leaves, the handle and spout applied, and the knob fixed on the lid. When we laughingly assured him that all handles had a trick of coming off, he gravely replied that this never happened with Dunmore ware, for the handles he put on never came off until the pot was broken – a statement we were inclined to believe after seeing how carefully he put them on.

[Bisque firing]
After the articles have reached this stage they are ready for biscuit firing, which occupies about 27 hours. From this they emerge biscuit-coloured, and with a rough or unglazed surface, and are bought in this state by ladies who wish to paint upon them [22].

[Glazing]
Those articles not intended to be left thus are now glazed and coloured. The colour is mixed with the glaze, and only an expert can tell what the result will be, the glaze bearing not the remotest resemblance to the hue it represents. For instance, a dash of pink paint comes out white, and red green, and so on in a most uncanny way. To the uninitiated eye this most important process is managed in the most casual way. A cheery old man, the father of our guide, was the dipper [23], and this is how he proceeded: – seizing a brush, he daubed on four spots of what looked like pink paint on the article intended to be glazed; then another four splashes of red (assuring us all the time it was white and green he was applying), and then plunged the pot into a

large tub of dark fluid – the glazing matter. From this it emerged dripping, but with no colour to be seen on it, ready for the glazing kiln.

[Glost firing]
There it has to remain sixteen hours, and at the end of that time comes out a lovely mottled, marled, spotted, or speckled article, to excite the admiration of all beholders.

Figure 42

Figure 43

LADY DUNMORE BOWL.

One very interesting feature of a pottery is that you never know what new effects may be produced, or what odd combinations of colouring. Everything is unpremeditated and original. Some of these effects may never be repeated again; and some are so quaint and so striking as to command fancy prices from people who like to possess artistic things. The kiln **[24]**, a circular building with a domed roof was receiving its next consignment of goods, and was supposed to be cool. Stepping in, I found it unpleasantly warm, and lost no time in retreating, though the fires had been off all Sunday and up to Monday afternoon **[25]**. When the furnace is in full blast the door is built up, and the articles subjected to intense heat.

[Display and Storage]
We came next to the showroom, where the finished goods are exhibited, showing all varieties, colourings, and designs of Dunmore pottery. The first thing which strikes the visitor is the marvellous variety of colouring **[26]** which can be attained in pottery – the deep solid hues, the opalescent conjunctions of dyes, the mottled, marled, crackled, crinkled, striped, spotted, and barred varieties of surface to be seen on every hand. There is deep red, ultramarine blue, a lovely revival of an old-fashioned tint; turquoise blue, a rare and expensive colour to produce; and sealing wax red, another new tint; greens of all shades; and yellows, from primrose to orange. One bronze-green vase had a most original effect. It was made of the new crackled ware, and the peculiar marking was most successfully carried out **[27]**.

The sketches throughout this article represent some of the more notable and artistic designs we saw here. When the Queen visited the Edinburgh Exhibition **[28]** she made extensive purchases of Dunmore ware, the turquoise blue and the light red and the new crackled ware being specially chosen by her. The vase

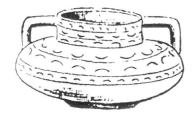

Figure 44

Figure 45

QUEEN'S VASE.

Figure 46

Figure 47

called the "Queen's Vase" **[29]** above was a shape she admired, and also the grotesque-looking stand for ferns called the "Dunmore Toad" **[30]** given below. The prettiest thing made of Dunmore ware we saw was a vase made to represent dark bronzed metal, with a band of dark red colouring traversed by the Greek key pattern in blue. Indeed, there is no end to the effects which may be produced by the potent agency of fire added to artistic taste and skill. In a glass case were a number of highly-finished articles showing the capacities of Dunmore ware. There were beautifully mottled tea sets, having the teapot and cream-jug mounted in silver **[31]**; an oval dish containing a pin-cushion, in which were stuck pins and brooches made of turquoise blue clay set in silver, and looking like a piece of enamel. Then there were terra-cotta plaques and vases painted with waxen-looking designs and fired, giving a most curious effect; and black and gold articles, with coloured designs *ad lib*. Some lovely brown tiles might

Figure 48

DUNMORE TOAD.

Figure 49

Figure 50

have been mistaken for mahogany, with natural streaks and markings; and other varieties of ware showed a conglomeration of colours which we were content to admire without attempting to describe, as no words would give any idea of their rich and strange effect. In the warehouse we were much puzzled at first by a continual crackling, ringing noise, which seemed to come from the pottery. It was, indeed, the ware contracting when coming into contact with the cold air, and this goes on for a long time after it leaves the kiln.

[Conclusion]

Very reluctantly we quitted this "house beautiful", and started through mud and mire for Larbert Station – a prosaic wind-up to the artistic experiences of our visit. The sketches which accompany the letterpress were kindly made by Mr J. W. Small, Stirling **[32]**.

Notes on the text of the 'Visit' Booklet

[1] Larbert Station

The reporter started the final leg of his journey to Dunmore Pottery at Larbert Station, whence shipments of Dunmore wares were probably dispatched, though due to the provision of railway services in the area, it perhaps only served as the actual loading point during the period 1848 to 1866, thereby predating the great era of production at Dunmore Pottery. Prior to that time, it could be that Dunmore Harbour was used for such a purpose, as it had been a thriving little port,

though it had suffered badly from the effects of Government cannon fire during the Jacobite Rebellion of 1745/6, after which the economy of Airth (town and parish) slumped dramatically. The harbour was still functioning in the 1920s, though nowadays it is all silted up (see Figure 51). Larbert Station was on the Scottish Central Railway line, running from Greenhill near Falkirk to Perth, via Stirling. It opened in 1848 and became very important to the rail network as a marshalling centre, and a

Figure 51

meeting point for railways from all over Scotland. Larbert Station (see Figure 52) was actually located at South Broomage, a quarter of a mile north-east of the town. From there, it was 3½ miles in a direct line to Dunmore Pottery, so the reporter's estimate of 4 miles by cab was very close to the mark. Larbert Station may have been the most convenient station for visitors to the Pottery, but it was not the closest. Two miles to the north, at a site in Pow's Wood designated Alloa Junction, the South Alloa branch was added, veering to the east and then heading northwards, terminating at South Alloa on the banks of the River Forth, whence a ferry took passengers across to Alloa Ferry Station to link up with the town of Alloa. It opened in 1852, if not earlier. This line passed very close to Dunmore Pottery, the nearest station being Carnock, almost a mile to the south (and a similar distance from Carnock Tower, which gave it its name).

Figure 52

There is a problem, here, however. Carnock Station is shown on the Ordnance Survey maps of 1859/60 (25-inch) and 1861 (6-inch), yet this does not tie in with information contained in the *Directory of Railway Stations*, where it is called Carnock Road Station, and stated not to have opened until January 1866; that same month, it was renamed Airth Road Station, and a year later, in

January 1867, the name was shortened to Airth, despite the station being all of a mile and three-quarters away from the town.[83] This is all very confusing, but it is unlikely to have had much impact on Dunmore Pottery at the time, as Peter Gardner had only recently taken over, and he was still some years away from transforming its fortunes.

In 1865, the Scottish Central Railway was absorbed by the Caledonian Railway, a much larger company, and it was to change the railway pattern of the area. Five years before the completion of its more famous counterpart, a railway bridge was opened across the Forth upriver of Alloa in 1885, thereby making the ferry crossing redundant. South Alloa Station was closed, and a new branch was created at Dunmore Junction, just over half a mile north of the Pottery, which looped westwards by Throsk to link up with the new swing-span bridge. The whole line from Alloa Junction to Alloa (West Junction) was now known as the Alloa Branch. It stayed open to passenger traffic until 1968, and Alloa Bridge remained operational until 1970, when it was fixed open and subsequently demolished. Airth Station (see Figure 53) functioned for something in the region of a century until it was eventually closed by British Railways in 1954.[84] This included the whole of Dunmore Pottery's most productive period, and so it may seem odd that it is the more distant Larbert Station which is mentioned in connection with the works. Perhaps Larbert (which is still in service), being on the main line, offered a more regular service, and the relative infrequency of trains on the branch line meant that it was more convenient for passengers (who could afford to) to alight at Larbert and complete their journey by cab, as the reporter did. This might also explain why Peter Gardner gave his address as "By Larbert" in the frontispiece to the *Visit* booklet, if he had the convenience of customers and visitors in mind. On the other hand, when he advertised Dunmore pottery in 1882, he informed potential customers that "The Works are within ten minutes' walk of Airth Station".[85] Additionally, it would no doubt have been advantageous to him to have used Airth Station rather than Larbert for the supply of raw

Figure 53

materials and the distribution of finished goods. An indication that this may have been occurring can be detected in the Valuation Rolls, for the address of Dunmore Pottery, linked with ground on the south side of Dunmore Moss, is given as "Airth Road Station" throughout the 1890s, which may be regarded as implying that Peter Gardner was making use of this station for commercial purposes. Even so, it must have been very frustrating for him to have had the railway line running a mere 70 yards from his Pottery yet having to endure a journey of close on a mile on a country back-road in order to dispatch his precious wares.

[2] Falkirk Tryst on Stennis Muir

A tryst can mean – among other things – an appointed meeting place, and a livestock market; both these concepts are inherent in the great Scottish trysts. The principal one was originally held at Crieff, but by the middle of the 18th century the amount of grazing land available to the large herds and flocks which were mustered there had been greatly reduced by the enclosure movement, large areas of former pasture being fenced off for cultivation. This resulted in the principal tryst being moved to the Falkirk area; it was originally located at Redding Muir until enclosures affected that area also, then it went to Roughcastle where old coal and iron workings proved too great a hazard, and finally in 1785 it settled at Stenhousemuir. The first part of the name – local pronunciation 'Stennis' – derives from 'stone house', which possibly refers to the mysterious (possibly Roman) stone structure known as Arthur's O'on, which was dismantled in 1743. In its heyday, 100,000 animals were sold at the Falkirk Tryst, and so it continued for over a hundred years. As the 19th century drew to an end, however, the Tryst was on the wane; new breeds of cattle were less able to make long journeys on the hoof, macadamised roads made it that much harder for them, tolls resulted in higher prices, better crop rotations provided winter fodder which meant that the huge autumn slaughter of beasts was no longer necessary, and finally the growth of the railways allowed animals to be transported easily and quickly in prime condition. By the 1920s the Falkirk Tryst was all but gone, though a flicker of the past still lives on today as a local fun-fair.[86]

(The description of the crowds on Stennis Muir given in the *Visit* booklet contains several words which may not be familiar to all readers, in which case notes 5 to 8 might prove helpful.)

[3] a Cruikshank

The reporter is here using a figure of speech called antonomasia: the substitution of the name of a famous person for a common noun, in order to designate a member of a group sharing the same basic characteristics. The person here must surely be George Cruikshank (1792-1878), an inventive caricaturist of high renown. He produced a work appropriate to the scene on Stennis Muir while still in his teens – a colourful frontispiece called 'The Beggars' Carnival' for Andrewes' *Dictionary of the Slang and Cant Languages*, 1809. A series of etchings entitled 'Points of Humour' illustrated comic passages from various anecdotes and legends, four of them coming from *The Jolly Beggars*; these were issued in two parts in 1823 and 1824. George Cruikshank was thus well known as an artist of droll and whimsical subjects some years before Victoria came to the throne, and he was to become the most famous political satirist of the Victorian era.

[4] a Doyle

Another example of antonomasia. There are two possibilities here, the first being Richard Doyle (1824-1883), one of whose most famous works was 'The Eglinton Tournament; or, Days of Chivalry revived', 1840. Two years later, he produced 'A Grand Historical, Allegorical, and Classical Procession', depicting a humorous and fanciful pageant. Alternatively, the reference in the booklet may be to his brother, Charles Altamont Doyle (1832-1893), who was also well known for his humorous sketches. A fine example is his 'Curling Match on Duddingston Loch' (see the Royal Caledonian Curling Club Christmas card for 1977).

[5] plaided

Plaided means to be clad in a plaid – a length of twilled woollen cloth, sometimes plain, sometimes chequered, but more usually having a tartan pattern, worn as a mantle or outer garment, predominantly in the rural areas of Scotland.

[6] mackintoshed

To be clad in a macintosh (no 'k'), named after Charles Macintosh (1766-1843), the celebrated inventor of a waterproof fabric from which countless millions of raincoats have been made. He took out his patent in 1823 and production began only months later, but there were initial problems caused by tailors, though unfamiliar with the new material, ignoring Macintosh's advice on how to make up waterproof garments. The factory therefore took over this task itself, and the 'macintosh' became almost universal. Although trade fell off somewhat with the widespread introduction of the railways, travellers not being exposed so much to the weather as they had been on stage coaches, the macintosh coat long remained the most popular of rainy-day apparel.

[7] ulstered

To be clad in an ulster, which was a long loose overcoat of frieze or other rough cloth, frequently worn with a waist belt. The 'Ulster overcoat' was introduced by J. C. McGhee & Co. of Belfast in 1867, and within a couple of years the abbreviated name was in common use.

[8] rung

In this context, a rung meant a stout stick, staff, or cudgel, which might be no more than the branch or bough of a tree.

[9] 'The Woods o' Dunmore'

This was the title of a romantic song which became popular just as the Victorian age was beginning. It was a baritone solo in G major, with lyrics by William Murdoch (1754-1839) and music by James Japp (1792-1860). It features in *The Auld Scotch Songs and Ballads* arranged and harmonised by Sinclair Dunn. He says: "This song appeared about sixty years ago [*i.e. ca.* 1835], and became a great favourite".[87] The opening verse goes thus:

This lone heart is thine, lassie, charming and fair,
This fond heart is thine, lassie dear;
Nae warlds's gear ha'e I, nae oxen nor kye,
I've naething, dear lassie, save a pure heart to gi'e;
Yet dinna say me na, but come, come awa',
An' wander, dear lassie, 'mang the woods o' Dunmore.

Those who went there without romance uppermost in mind could appreciate the arboreal variety provided by this area of woodland, which supported birch, oak, ash, elm, beech, and fir (according to the *Old Statistical Account* of the parish of Airth), though the area certainly had romantic possibilities. "In summer, the foliage of the trees everywhere forms a 'bosky umbrage' [area of

Figure 54

unfrequented leafy shade], grandly variegated. As seen from the neighbouring straths, the woods display a spread of hues changeful as the colours of harlequin's coat".[88] It might possibly have been the reporter's reference to this song in the *Visit* booklet which prompted Peter Gardner to produce one of his most amusing animal pieces. He created the figure of a frog, head thrown right back and singing lustily (see Figure C1), clutching in its forefeet a sheet of music headed 'The Woods o' Dunmore' and including four lines of musical notes! (see Figure 54). Some other amusing froggy items are shown adjacent (see Figures C2 and C3). There were, incidentally, at least two more romantic songs which were inspired by this locality: 'The Maid of Dunmore' told of an imprisoned lass who was rescued by her lover, and 'The Rose of Dunmore' was about another lass whose lover was away fighting with Admiral Nelson.

[10] Mr Gardner

This was Peter Gardner, master potter, the man responsible for radically altering the nature of the wares produced at Dunmore Pottery so that it achieved lasting fame. For details, see the Frontispiece, section I.

[11] the foreman / guide

In all, the booklet describes four workers in sufficient detail to enable their names to be put forward tentatively as a result of information contained in the Census Returns (see Appendix A). This man reappears later in the narrative (see note 21).

[12] clay from England

This clay source is confirmed by Arnold Fleming, who visited Dunmore Pottery in the course of gathering information for his book. He wrote: "Not content with the local clay, Gardner still further improved his ware by bringing clay from Cornwall and Devon".[89] This is not to say that the local clay lacked the quality necessary to produce first-rate pottery, as Fleming readily admits:

"He [Peter Gardner] began by putting the fine red clay to a better and higher artistic use than had formerly been attempted, with the result that Dunmore became a flourishing pottery".[90] Fleming was clearly impressed by what Peter Gardner could achieve using locally-won material: "the rich pure copper-green glaze on the red terra-cotta ware was very effective".[91] Being able to acquire clay from South-West England allowed greater flexibility of production, and permitted him to expand his range of ware, though it should be remembered that this new source supplemented rather than supplanted his local supply, and on occasions the two were actually worked in concert, as the following note demonstrates.

[13] striped goods

Here the booklet is doubtless referring to agate ware, which is produced by wedging (kneading) blocks of different coloured clays together, and throwing the resultant lump on the wheel as a single ball. Minimal wedging will leave large single-coloured areas, whereas prolonged wedging will result in a much greater mingling of the colours. As russet red and creamy white are the normal colours of clay used, a well-wedged piece can assume the appearance of natural agate, though only after the turner has taken away the skin of slurry. The prime exponent of this technique was the Seaton Pottery in Aberdeen under the Gavins. Agate ware can also be produced by press moulding after wedging, though the result gives a more rigidly banded effect. This technique was preferred by Belfield of Prestonpans. The clay could also be artificially coloured, such as the pastel blues, pinks, greens, and greys employed by Cochran & Fleming of the Britannia Pottery in Glasgow. All of these factories operated during the Dunmore period. The excitement of the technique, and the intriguing results which it can produce, also attracted the interest of craft potters of the later 20th century, most notably Alasdair Dunn on the Isle of Arran. Agate ware is essentially different from marbled ware, to which it may have a superficial resemblance, the latter being achieved by pouring lines of creamy slip onto a russet body and joggling it about, creating a quasi-agate appearance – but only on the surface. (Beware: some reference books reverse these terms, and to make matters more confusing, in a culinary context, a cake mix following the 'agate' principle produces a 'marble' cake!)

Dunmore Pottery did indeed produce agate ware (marked examples are not uncommon), and, as the booklet relates, the wedging of the local red clay with imported white clay would suit this purpose very well. It must be said, however, that the technique was used in a way which produced a form of stripy banding rather lacking in visual impact. Remarkably, it was often made even less striking by the curious decision to disguise the agate effect by the application of semi-opaque running glazes – surely an example of 'gilding the lily' (see Figure C11). There was another unexpected use of agate ware at Dunmore: the making of kiln separators. These consisted of roughly-formed strips of extruded clay, more or less circular in section and cut into short lengths, which were used to keep items from becoming fused to the inside of their saggers or to the kiln shelving. Separators discovered on the Dunmore site are usually made of either russet-red clay or white clay; those of agate (for which there is no decorative justification) were presumably produced from the leftovers after a session of throwing agate ware pots.[92]

[14] the potter's wheel

It is clear from the account that throwing was done on a traditional style of hand-powered wheel. Such a wheel is illustrated by Arnold Fleming in his book *Scottish Pottery*, and that drawing is reproduced here (see Figure 55). Fleming describes it as "primitive" in his 1923 caption, not just because of its simplicity, but also because of the motive power source as described in the *Visit* booklet, and it is no surprise to learn that in the big-city factories, "Manual[ly] driven wheels have now given place to steam power".[93] Indeed, the process had been under way for decades in the larger factories, but traditional ways still persisted at Dunmore in the late 1880s.

Figure 55

[15] potting referred to in old books

It is difficult to guess what the reporter had in mind when talking of "the oldest of books". In terms of proto-books, the oldest would be the papyrus rolls of ancient Egypt, or the clay tablets of the Sumerians, Babylonians, Assyrians, and Hittites; both date from about 3000 BC. In the third century BC, the Chinese made books out of bamboo strips bound together with cords. China created something closer to a conventional book in AD 175, when Confucian texts began to be carved into stone tablets and preserved in the form of rubbings. The Greeks adopted the papyrus roll and passed it on to the Romans, but by AD 400 it had been superseded by the vellum or parchment codex (manuscript volume), which may be regarded as the first true form of book. The printing of books (which would define a book in modern terms) was being practiced in China in the 6th century, using lampblack on wooden blocks, with Europe employing the printing press from the 15th century onwards. To name the oldest book which mentions the making of pottery would be a most difficult task, but perhaps that is not what the reporter meant by "the oldest of Books" (and the clue lies in the capitalisation of the initial letter of the last word) – it could be regarded as a cryptic expression meaning the Bible.[94] There are indeed a number of references to potters in the Bible, mostly in the metaphorical sense *e.g.* "I have raised up one from the north, and he shall come: from the rising of the sun shall he call upon my name: and he shall come upon princes as upon mortar, and as the potter treadeth clay".[95] It sounds as if the task of the potter preparing his clay for the wheel was regarded as an act of dependable certainty, with the wedging in this case being done by foot rather than by hand. Another entry seems to suggest that there was a royal guild of potters in Old Testament times: "These were the potters, and those that dwelt among plants and hedges: there they dwelt with the king for his work".[96] Because of the nature of pottery production, particularly the necessity to fire the wares in a kiln, potters tended to be a lot less itinerant than many other craftsmen were in olden times, and it is therefore odd that the above-quoted verse makes them sound nomadic, or at least of no fixed abode. The truth of the statement that there were potters producing goods for royalty is confirmed by sherds which have been found bearing impressed marks stating (in translation) 'Belonging to the King'. Perhaps the most telling entry in the Bible comes from the book of Jeremiah:[97]

> The word which came to Jeremiah from the Lord, saying
> 2 Arise, and go to the potter's house, and there I will cause thee to hear my words.
> 3 Then I went down to the potter's house, and, behold, he wrought a work on the wheels. [It is interesting that the last word is in the plural, for it indicates that the historical context of this passage would probably have been after the Exodus. Around that time, the single wheel rotating around a vertical shaft was supplemented by a second, larger disc, mounted below the first. This speeded up the rate of turning, and the task of keeping it moving may have been the duty of a potter's assistant. By this means, production would have been considerably increased.]
> 4 And the vessel that he made of clay was marred in the hand of the potter: so he made it again another vessel, as seemed good to the potter to make it.
> 5 Then the word of the Lord came to me, saying
> 6 O house of Israel, cannot I do with you as this potter? saith the Lord. Behold, as the clay is in the potter's hand, so are ye in my hand, O house of Israel.

The purpose of this passage may have been to provide a metaphorical parallel, but verses 3 and 4 give an account of the actual potting process, which is perhaps what the reporter had in mind.

[16] potting depicted in Egyptian paintings
The reporter clearly had quite a wide range of knowledge concerning ceramic matters, and seems to have been keen to present this to his readers. There are many pictorial representations of pottery making in Ancient Egypt, one of the best being the painted frieze in shallow relief from the Mastaba of Ti at Saqqara (see Figure 56). It dates from about 2350 BC, late in the Vth dynasty; it had been discovered in 1860, and so could possibly have been known to the reporter. The frieze may be divided into four scenes.[98]

(a) On the far left is a large, biconical kiln, which appears to have a dozen bonts (strengthening hoops). The top seems to have been closed over with a dome of clay. In front of the kiln a man is sitting on the ground; he is protecting his face against the heat with his right hand, while with his left he is regulating the air intake by holding a lid in front of the firehole. (Although not shown in this sketch, the firehole appears in photographs under a small arch.[99] The artist who made the sketch did not appreciate its significance.) No clothing is apparent on the man. The hieroglyphics may be translated as 'heating the kiln'.

(b) Next, there is a man sitting on a low support; with his right hand he is turning a potter's wheel, while with his left he is fashioning the rim of a restricted (closed-form) bowl. He is dressed in a garment resembling female attire, which may be a form of apron, perhaps to protect his body from being smeared with slurry. The hieroglyphics may be translated as '*hnw*-vessels are fashioned'; two more of these distinctive bowls can be seen above and to the left, positioned under a row of vases.

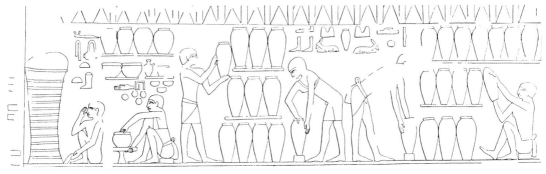

Figure 56

(c) In the centre of the frieze, two men are depicted working with large restricted vases. The man on the right is leaning over such a vessel which he has placed on a low support, and is holding the rim between the fingers of his right hand, while with his left he may be burnishing it. His attitude suggests that he is pressing the vessel down on the support to keep it stable while he performs the polishing motion. Although no tool is evident, he must surely have been using one, probably made of stone, bone, or wood. He is wearing a similar apron-like garment to the man in the previous scene. The other man, on the left, is seen holding up one of these large vases, supporting it underneath with his left hand and keeping it steady with his right. He may be inspecting it, or perhaps he is simply adding it to the rows of similar vessels, probably for drying. He is wearing the normal Egyptian kilt-type garment. The hieroglyphics may be translated as '*dwiw*-vessels glitter', no doubt a reference to the shiny, polished surface produced by burnishing.

(d) The final scene again shows two men working with the same type of large restricted vases. The man on the left has adopted a similar attitude to the adjacent man in the previous scene, and the pot on which he is working is likewise supported on the same type of low support. While the steadying hand is also in the same position, the other hand is not; by contrast, this man is working not on the rim but on the interior of the jar. His job would appear to be less messy than that of the previous man, and he wears the simple kilt garment. The other man in the scene, who is similarly attired, is sitting on a low support, and he is also working on the interior of one of these large vases, only this time he is holding it up in an inverted position. Many other similar pots have already been completed. The hieroglyphics may be translated as 'fashioning *dwiw*-vessels'.

Just how close all this is to the Egyptian paintings which the reporter had in mind is hard to say; likewise it is not easy to assess the extent of its relevance to pottery production at Dunmore. Nonetheless, it is indicative of the many common threads which run through the craft of potting in all countries during all periods.

[17] potting demonstrated at the Colonial Exhibition
The event referred to is the Colonial and Indian Exhibition, London 1886. It was held at South Kensington, and opened by Queen Victoria on 4th May. It became known colloquially as the Colinderies. The reporter seems to imply that there was a "mild Hindoo" actually engaged in making pottery at this Exhibition, and so there was. The art ware courts were arranged along ethnic / geographic lines, with divisions and subdivisions of different wares within each. Most featured pottery, both glazed and unglazed, ranging from sophisticated to fairly crude. However, the working potter was not to be found here, but in the Palace. The catalogue explains: "Previous Exhibitions have served to illustrate some of the multitudinous arts and products of our Indian Empire, but it has been left for this occasion to bring before us the technical processes of their manufactures". To achieve this, a Palace Durbar Hall was constructed of carved wood, "and in connection with it the peculiar feature of most Oriental Palaces, a *karkhaneh*, or workshop, where jewellers, weavers, carvers, and others would carry on their trades, and produce before the visitors the marvellous and beautiful objects of their handiwork".[100] It is disappointing that potting was not specifically mentioned, and the same omission occurred in the account which appeared in the *Art Journal* of that year: "In the outer courtyard [of the Indian Palace] are a number of small workshops, in which brightly-costumed Indian artificers weave, carve, do metal-work, and carry on a variety of trades".[101] In all, 37 artisans were engaged here, having been selected by, and working under the charge of, Dr Tyler of Agra. They were drawn from 10 cities, the greatest number (8) coming from Agra, which lies in the modern state of Uttar Pradesh in north-central India (the most populous state in the Indian Union, where Hinduism is one of the main religions). Among these working craftsmen, there was indeed a potter, and we even have his name; he was called Bakshiram, and he had attained the remarkable age of 102 years.

The same scene could be appreciated by visitors to the Glasgow International Exhibition of 1888 (which would appear to have taken place after the publication of the *Visit* booklet), which a reviewer of the Exhibition described thus: "At the western extremity of the Indian Court may be seen the Indian potter at work with his simple and primitive implements and appliances, just as his ancestors before him in the village communities of India exercised their craft for a period of probably not less that two thousand years. His apparatus is of a rude and clumsy enough character, consisting of a heavy wheel or table, mounted on a pivot, to which he gives motion by jerking with his hand".[102] The article identifies him as a Hindoo, and contrasts his rudimentary method of potting with the mechanised techniques of Messrs. Doulton, which were also on show at the Exhibition.

[18] the thrower
The only operation in the entire sequence of making a pot to be illustrated in the *Visit* booklet is that of throwing on the wheel – hardly surprising, perhaps, that it should be singled out in this

way, as it is a very evocative process, and the one most closely identified in the public mind as representing the making of a pot. The potter (see Figure 35) is shown as a sturdily-built man, bearded and bonneted. He has his sleeves rolled up, and he is wearing some form of apron across his chest, or it could be an overall garment such as dungarees, which was the standard working attire for potters in the industrial factories. Some jobs in a pottery were too hot for comfort (as the *Visit* booklet recounted), but that of the thrower was not one of them, and headgear was generally worn, particularly in the winter months. Again, the peaked cap was fairly standard. The back support, which is indicated in the sketch, signifies that the operative sitting here is a production potter, who would generally be at the wheel for the full working day. Such a fitting would afford a momentary respite between each throwing. The wheel itself appears to be sitting on a triangular structure which has no sides above wheel level; this is unusual, as the absence of such a fitting (known as the slurry box) would allow the spread of the inevitable mess which accompanies the throwing of pots because of the essential aqueous lubricant used by the potter. There is a disappointing absence of tools, and the all-important water bowl. The only device other than the wheel to be shown is a short vertical stanchion with a semi-circular horizontal fixing. This could be a device to hold gauges – adjustable prongs with whalebone tips whereby a production potter can regulate size and shape during a run of a single type of vessel by keeping a couple of key measurements constant. Perhaps the artist considered them too finicky to show in a thumb-nail sketch such as this. There is just a hint of the other essential concomitant of a potter's wheel, and that is the power-source to make it revolve; boxing, disappearing to the left, doubtless holds the belts which convey the power from the turning wheel which is driven by the thrower's assistant. The text says that these two artisans "work in closest harmony", and the assistant had an additional incentive for performing to the satisfaction of the thrower, for it was he, and not the company cashier, who paid the wages of his helpers. Although a team of two worked at throwing the pots at Dunmore, it was often the case that three people were involved in this process – one to prepare the clay, one to turn the wheel, and one to do the potting. This is beautifully illustrated on a terra-cotta plaque sculpted by Wallace Martin of the Southall Pottery in London.[103] The situation as described at Dunmore indicates that no-one was specifically allocated to the first of these tasks (the operative being known as a bencher, because they wedged the clay on a bench before weighing it and balling it up in readiness for the thrower). In factories, where the motive power for the potter's wheel was mechanical, it was the bencher and the thrower who formed the team of two.

The attitude of the potter shown in the sketch is not altogether convincing. It is instructive to compare it with a present-day production thrower – the problem is to find one, as the era of industrial pottery production in Scotland is all but extinct. Fortunately, there is one man left, who may be regarded as a lone survivor. Joe Hunter worked at the Govancroft Pottery in Glasgow until its closure in 1982; he then transferred to A.W. Buchan & Co. at Crieff, whither it had moved ten years previously upon leaving its home in Portobello. He worked for the company until it folded in 1999, and he still continues to keep the name of the Thistle Pottery alive in one part of the former factory. The attitude of Joe Hunter while throwing is very different from that of the Dunmore potter (see Figure 36). He bends over his work to a far greater extent and watches intently as he develops the shape of the pot he is creating. By contrast, the Dunmore potter is sitting well back, almost touching the back-rest, and does not appear even to be looking at his handiwork. By placing *both* hands on the pot in such a fashion, he is not doing any actual work. For these reasons, it is Joe Hunter's opinion that the potter in the sketch is posing for the artist. So who might this potter be? It is tempting to think that it could be Peter Gardner himself. He was, after all, too busy to show his visitors round the works, and after receiving the reporter and the sketch artist, he passed them over to his foreman to take them on a tour of the Pottery. Could it be that he reckoned his time was better spent on the wheel? If it is not Peter Gardner who appears in the sketch, it is unlikely that we will ever know who it is. The Census Returns specify three Dunmore potters as throwers, but they appear rather too early to be considered as candidates here, whereas in the closest Censuses to the *Visit*, those of 1881 and 1891, half a dozen workers are given the simple designation "potter" without further clarification. This man may have to remain anonymous.

[19] the turner

He is described as being an old man with traces of a Derbyshire accent, which makes it fairly straightforward to identify him as William Harrison. The Census Returns reveal only two Dunmore potters who were born in England. One was this man, who was born in 1829, making him around 58 years old at this time (and who therefore should have been described, at the most, as elderly rather than old); the other was Thomas Harrison, who at 31 could not merit such a description. Crucially, William Harrison is described as being a "Pottery Turner" in 1881. It is possible that before coming to Dunmore, he had worked at Alloa Pottery, as his four children were all born in that town in the period 1868-72.

[20] the moulder

The reporter points out that in the production of teapots, which is clearly of major importance to the Pottery, the body and the lid are thrown, whereas the spout, handle, and knob are moulded. This latter task is performed by a girl, and this could possibly be Jane Campbell (though at the age of 26, she would have been better described as a young woman). In 1881, she is listed simply as a "Pottery Worker"; but we also have Isabella Campbell, who would have been aged 51 by this time and therefore in no sense a girl, named ten years earlier as a "Spout Maker in Pottery". It is tempting to think of this as an example of a mother passing on her skills to her daughter. A daily output of two gross gives an indication of the popularity of Dunmore teapots.

[21] the fixer

This highly-skilled job might have been the responsibility of James Campbell, who in 1871 was listed as a "Presser & Mould Maker", and he could have moved on to the rather trickier task of fixing. His wife was Isabella Campbell, the spout maker, which offers the intriguing possibility of not one but both parents passing on their combined skills to their daughter (actually, adopted daughter) Jane. If correct, this also gives us the name of the foreman at Dunmore Pottery (see note 11).

[22] bisqueware lady decorators

It was not an uncommon practice for potteries to release goods in a bisque-fired condition to be decorated by people quite unconnected with the works. They could be amateur or professional, female or male. Methven of Kirkcaldy did this to a considerable extent, and even Wemyss Ware was treated in this fashion, though perhaps only at the time of its closure (*ca.* 1930). The odd fact is that these were not special production runs, reserved exclusively for that purpose, but such pieces generally seem to have been taken out of the normal stock and therefore often carried the impressed maker's mark, which could lure the unwary into a false understanding of the decorative style of the named potworks. Perhaps a more appropriate parallel is the Seaton Pottery in Aberdeen, which regularly made large redware vases (known colloquially as 'Rebecca jars') upon which local artists could try their skills. It seems that Dunmore Pottery indulged in the same practise, exclusively for ladies according to the account. While the white earthenware of Kirkcaldy was glazed after such decoration, the red earthenware of the potteries at Dunmore, Aberdeen, and Errol was not, and therefore the paintwork is very susceptible to chipping. It could be that the decorators acquired their pots direct from the works, or they could have purchased them from an intermediary. If the latter was the case, we have a likely candidate: Peter Duncan of 27 Port Street, Stirling. There he ran glass and china warerooms, and although an advertisement of 1882 mentions a wide range of the pottery which he purveyed, it unfortunately does not specify Dunmore ware; it does, however, mention "Terra-Cotta [bisque-fired redware] for Painting".[104] The booklet also resolves the seeming paradox with regard to the term 'biscuit', for *bis cuit* in French means 'twice cooked', whereas biscuit ware has been fired only once. However, it refers not to the sequence of operations, but to the colour of the unglazed body after a single firing.

[23] the dipper

He is described as being a cheery old man, the father of the guide, whom it is reckoned was James Campbell. The Census Returns indicate that the dipper was John Campbell, who, at 74 years of age, had certainly earned the epithet 'old' as applied to a person still working, engaged in an industrial process. With an age gap of 22 years, it is quite feasible that they were father and son, the elder coming from Portobello and the younger from Duddingston; the two townships are adjacent to each other, to the north-east of Edinburgh, which adds to the likelihood. John Campbell is described as a "Pottery Fireman" in 1871 (*i.e.* in charge of stoking the kiln), and simply as a "Potter" in 1881. The very responsible job of firing pottery, especially the glost firing, would no doubt have entailed an intimate knowledge of glazes, and as the years began to catch up with him, he might have been given a physically less-demanding job which would still have benefited from his experience as a fireman. If this was the case, then some credit should accrue to John Campbell for assisting in the production of the wonderful glazes which characterise so much of the output of this Pottery.

[24] the kiln

Generally the most visible feature of any pottery, it is the kiln which most characterises the enterprise as a potworks. The longevity of the Dunmore kiln, and its eventual demise, give it a special place in Scottish pottery history, and it merits special treatment here: see Appendix B.

[25] unpleasantly warm

A degree of romanticism has accrued around the notion of working in a pottery, and while this may be true to a degree with occupations such as that of the thrower, it should not be forgotten that in terms of industrial pottery production, many of the jobs were concerned with hard physical labour. One of the least popular tasks was drawing (emptying) a kiln of wares as soon after firing as the slowly-diminishing heat level would allow. On the occasion of the reporter's visit, this job had already been completed and the kiln was being set (stacked) in preparation for its next firing. Well over 24 hours had elapsed since the previous firing had been completed, the kiln had been emptied of its finished wares and was in the process of receiving its new consignment, and yet still the reporter, almost as soon as he stepped inside, was compelled to beat a hasty retreat. There is no suggestion that Peter Gardner was anything but a benevolent employer, but the same could not have been said for every one of the proprietors of the large city factories, and those workers employed in this particular task had to endure conditions which would not have survived scrutiny in relation to health and safety regulations of later times. These circumstances were recorded by Peter Denholm (well known for his excavation of the Clyde Pottery at Greenock) when witnessing what was probably the last coal-firing at an industrial pottery in Britain, which took place at Longton, Staffordshire, in 1978. "During the cooling time we heard many stories current among local potter families, of how some pottery managers of old, anxious to have orders delivered, would send their men into the kiln to draw the wares while it was still much too hot for health; although they went in covered with wet cloths, many were the singed scalps and scorched backs, and for anyone who refused it was 'out in the street' with a curse, no insurance cover, and lucky if they had a week's pay in lieu of notice".[105] Such a situation doubtless pertained in some of the Scottish factories as well.

[26] the marvellous variety of colouring

It is clear that the reporter was impressed by all aspects of production at Dunmore, but at the end of the tour the most memorable effect was that created by colour – a further testimony to the appeal of Peter Gardner's wondrous glazes. It may therefore be worth summarising the various colours specifically mentioned in the account:

> deep red, ultramarine blue, turquoise blue, sealing-wax red, greens of all shades, and yellows from primrose to orange.

In addition, there was:

> bronze-green (for crackled ware);
> black and gold, with coloured designs *ad.lib.* [Latin *ad libitum*, meaning 'at pleasure'];
> brown which might have been mistaken for mahogany, with (quasi-)natural streaks and markings;

and "the prettiest thing made of Dunmore ware which we saw":

> a vase made to represent dark bronzed metal, with a band of dark red colouring traversed by the Greek key pattern in blue.

The latter item sounds quite splendid; the pity is that at the time of writing, no example bearing this particular colour scheme has yet come to light. Two factors must be borne in mind regarding the above list of colours: firstly, it is far from complete, and secondly, it was not just the individual colours which made Dunmore ware so special, but the spectacular way in which they were so often combined. It is also worth recalling what Arnold Fleming had to say about this subject in *Scottish Pottery*. He picked out three colours for particular mention: (i) "a deep rich Mazarine blue, greatly admired by collectors"; (ii) "the rich pure copper-green glaze on the red terra-cotta ware was very effective, and rivalled the green glazes produced by such eminent potters in Staffordshire as the Mintons"; (iii) "the crimson glaze was also very rich, and had a soft deep luscious tint".[106] Fleming was especially impressed by Peter Gardner's control of glazes: "All these coloured glazes had to be fired with great care, and a vast amount of attention was required, not only in glazing and handling the articles, but also in managing the assortment in the kiln so that one colour would not strike or injure another. For example, blues are very apt to stain all other articles in the same sagger blue. So also, copper is a metal that strikes the inside of the sagger, and will injure whatever is put in the same sagger in future firings. But Gardner [corrected spelling] saw to it that the whole style of the ware was suited to this difficulty in the use of coloured glazes".[107] On the specific subject of merging colours, he had this to say: "The rustic dessert services, representing all kinds of leaves and fruits as well as different animals, were arrived at by splashing various tints of brown, yellow and green glazes on the surface of the ware".[108] As his palette of glazes expanded, Gardner was able to produce spectacular combinations of splashed colouring on his pots (for an example, see Figure C24).

[27] the new crackled ware

Using the word 'new' enables the introduction of this most distinctive ware to be placed in the mid 1880s. The basic colour, as the reporter notes, is bronze-green, but it is the crackled glaze effect which gives these items their special appeal. Crazing is a defect, and excessive crazing would render a piece of pottery unsaleable and therefore represent a production failure – unless it was deliberately executed in such a way that it resulted in an intriguing decorative feature. Such was the case here, though it must be remembered that Peter Gardner did not invent this technique, for the craquelure effect was popular in China in the 18th century. It has long been recognised that he had a fondness for Chinese shapes, a number of Dunmore items making no attempt to conceal their Chinese origins in terms of the source of the designer's inspiration. Indeed, some pieces may have been cast from moulds made directly from Chinese originals (for an example, see Figure C28). Some of the glaze colours, too, have Chinese overtones; the deep red and the turquoise blue, for instance, were popular with the potters of the Kangxi period during the Q'ing Dynasty (1662-1722). It would seem that in terms of glazing techniques, the Dunmore crackled ware has strong echoes of Chinese ceramic art. It may also be compared with the craquelure products of Sir Edmund Elton of the Sunflower Pottery at Clevedon Court in Somerset. The gold and silver (actually platinum) crackling effect was rendered even more dramatically than at Dunmore, though these products were somewhat later, dating from the period 1902-1910. Most of Gardner's products of this type accentuate the crazing by giving it a pale green tint which stands out in sharp contrast to the dark green body of the pot (see Figure C9). Sometimes an even more dramatic effect was created by featuring an orange craquelure against a pea-green body, giving a most spectacular result (see Figure C10). The craquelure effect is achieved when two colours are combined which have different rates of thermal expansion and contraction.

[28] the Edinburgh Exhibition

This refers to the Edinburgh International Exhibition of Industry, Science, and Art, 1886. Dunmore Pottery made its mark in several ways, and the topic is of sufficient importance to merit an article in its own right. This appears as Appendix C.

[29] the 'Queen's Vase'

As the appendix article mentioned immediately above discusses, Queen Victoria (who was Patron of the Edinburgh International Exhibition) took a fancy to Peter Gardner's products. The text of the *Visit* booklet, in the sentence immediately following the reference to the Edinburgh Exhibition, describes the 'Queen's Vase' as "a shape she admired", and it is illustrated immediately above (see Figure 44), the implication being that she particularly admired it when she saw it in the Exhibition, and it was probably among the pieces which she purchased. However, there is a slight conundrum here. At the time of writing, no piece of Dunmore pottery has been found which corresponds exactly with this shape, and so the photograph which sits beside the contemporary sketch is of a vase which is similar, but not identical (see Figures 45 and C7). Both are broad and squat, and both have very wide strap handles which rise almost vertically from the body and turn through approximately 90° before joining the neck on the horizontal. There are differences too, though: the centre of gravity of the vase in the photograph is considerably lower, and the handles are flush with the top of the neck, whereas in the sketch they appear to be fixed just below it. Furthermore, the Queen's Vase is shown to have a considerable amount of moulded decoration which is absent from the various examples examined of the shape shown in the photograph, though one has been seen with a sprigged-on relief pattern. The contrasting coloration of the dribbled glazes may give a vague impression of texturing, but it certainly cannot be mistaken for the regular bands of decoration which are clearly shown in the sketch. Although uncommon, Dunmore Pottery did produce hand-textured wares such as this. A vase has been noted with a globular body and a long slimmish neck, carrying a deep red glaze verging on black in places, which has turned grooves and large impressed dots. Ironically, exactly the same body shape as depicted in the photograph is also known to have been made by another factory, the Fife Pottery of Robert Heron & Son in Kirkcaldy (though with a much narrower neck and steeply rising handles). A sketch of it appears in an early catalogue of Wemyss Ware shapes, and is reproduced beside the photograph for comparison (see Figure 46). An item with a shape which is perhaps closer to the Queen's Vase is known to have been made at Dunmore. The general proportion is certainly more akin to the item in the booklet sketch, but the carination (ridged change of body angle) is too abrupt, and, most noticeably, the handles go through two right-angled bends instead of one (see Figure 47). Some examples have a plain glaze while others are highly mottled, but although the latter instance provides a general effect which is closer to the patterning evident in the sketched booklet version, it still lacks the regularity of what surely must be a moulded pattern. The search for a convincing 'Queen's Vase' continues.

[30] the 'Dunmore Toad'

Dunmore Pottery is widely renowned for its zoömorphic shapes, with frogs and toads being much in favour. Many of these items perform floral functions – cute little frogs as posy vases, large flat-bodied warty toads as wall-mounted receptacles for sprays. Most are amusing, none more so than the frog which so lustily sings 'The Woods o' Dunmore' (see Figure C1 and note no. 9). There is one shape, however, generally known as *the* Dunmore Toad, which is of a slightly more menacing nature (see Figures 48, 49, and C8). Far from being natural, or even a caricature of nature, it is somewhat grotesque, and remarkable for only having three legs. This weird creature is no figment of Peter Gardner's imagination, but rather another example of the way in which he was influenced by Chinese art. The three-legged toad was an important figure in Chinese mythology, and later it occupied a similar role in Japan. Its significance lay primarily in Taoist philosophy, in which it often accompanies one of the eight immortals: Liu Hai, the god of wealth (in consequence of which, it is often depicted with a copper coin in its mouth – but not at Dunmore). The three-legged toad is also known as the Moon Toad because of the Chinese claim to be able to trace its outline on the moon. Figure 50 shows what is said to be a Chinese prototype of the Dunmore Toad, the main difference between them resulting from the making technique, hand-modelling as opposed to moulding, which allows the creation of protruding eye-balls and upstanding eye-lashes on the Chinese example. Similar features are also apparent on an English version, made by Burmantofts Pottery in Leeds, which produced a range of art pottery between 1881 and 1904 not dissimilar in terms of both shapes and glazes to some of the Dunmore wares. Their Chinese moon toad, made for use as a plant or fern pot, was described as "Burmantofts' Grotesque Monster", and appears in catalogues issued by Liberty's in 1891, though "design probably mid-1880s",[109] according to the local museum. On the subject of grotesques, aspects of Dunmore zoömorphic humour may be seen in the works of the Martin Brothers of the Southall Pottery in London (1873-1914), who took the subject to grotesque extremes.

[31] pottery mounted in silver

Very occasionally, items of pottery were provided with silver mountings. Presumably this was only done when requested by important and/or wealthy customers. The Port Dundas Pottery in Glasgow is known to have had items of decorative salt-glazed stoneware embellished in this way, and Dunmore Pottery did likewise (an example is illustrated here; see Figure C12 – the hallmarks include the date-stamp for 1882/3). Of course, the fixing of silver mountings is not part of the pottery production process and so could be done at a later date. It is therefore interesting to read in the *Visit* booklet that such an operation was apparently performed at the Pottery.

[32] Small's sketches

The reporter had the foresight to be accompanied by an illustrator, working in concert, so that the verbal account is given the occasional boost of being accompanied by a visual image. The text at one point says: "The sketches throughout this article represent some of the more notable and artistic designs we saw here". It must be admitted that most of the sketches have little artistic merit, but they are sufficient to give an impression of a range of Dunmore items which were in current production at the time when the article/booklet was being written. In all, ten pieces of Dunmore ware are shown:

a tall pedestalled vase inside a giant O which is the initial letter of the text;

a group of four bowls and vases, all very different in shape, which apper above a line of the running text which has the appearance of acting as a caption, and although it says "moulded by a few deft touches", throwing would seem to be the fundamental process involved with most of them;

then come three items which are all captioned in the conventional sense, being the Lady Dunmore Bowl, the Dunmore Toad, and the Queen's Vase, all of which are discussed separately elsewhere in this booklet (the first one also appears on the frontispiece);

and finally there is a naturalistic owl, and a large bowl resembling a half-opened lotus flower.

In addition to these various items of pottery, there is also a sketch of a potter at work on the wheel, as discussed in the note on the thrower (no.18 above).

The very last sentence in the booklet identifies the illustrator: "The sketches which accompany the letterpress were kindly made by Mr J. W. Small, Stirling". Even allowing for their thumb-nail quality – of necessity, it may be imagined, if they were done 'on the hoof', as it were – they do not signify the work of a notable sketch artist. Perhaps the worst instance is the nature of the fixing of the handles of the Queen's Vase, both to the neck and to the body, where the precise arrangement is not apparent. On the other hand, the complexities of the Lady Dunmore bowl are well handled, the owl has a humorous expression of which Peter Gardner himself would surely have approved, and the group of four carry an air of gracefulness. All in all, the sketches represent a creditable artistic effort, and provide a valuable visual record with which to supplement the text. The artist is probably John W. Small (1851-1930), who was by profession an architect, and lived in Forth Street, Stirling. There is every likelihood that he is the same John W. Small who had previously lived in Edinburgh at 16 Caledonian Place, calling himself an architect for the first time in 1877, and establishing his practice at 56 George Street in 1878. He had several works on display at the Royal Scottish Academy between 1880 and 1883. By 1884 he is no longer listed in the Edinburgh Post Office Directories; it appears that he moved to Stirling, and joined the Stirling Fine Art Association. They held exhibitions in the Smith Institute (now Art Gallery & Museum) and the name of John W. Small features in several of the catalogues, dated 1891, 1894, 1897, and 1900 (on two occasions). The *Dictionary of Scottish Painters* records that he was a watercolour artist who specialised in architectural views of Stirling and other towns in the area, and flourished in the period 1880-1900,[110] and so a date of 1887 for these sketches fits in very nicely with his career. In view of the fact that sketching was not his speciality, Small's illustrations in the *Visit* booklet represent a commendable effort. To be fair to John Small, he was a draftsman of meticulous skill, and he was no doubt under pressure that day to keep up with the pace of the reporter. Irrespective of the artistic quality of his sketches, they are of considerable value in the historical sense.

Appendix A

Dunmore Potters in Census Returns

1841 Census

Head of the Pottery was John Gardner, the address simply being Dunmore Pottery. His age is given as 40, though this is too low by two or three years (it seemingly being the practice in the 1841 Census for adults to have their ages rounded down to the nearest multiple of five years). With him was his second wife Helen (38) [his first wife, Janet, having died in 1828] and their children Margaret (9), Peter (7), Helen (4), and Anne (1). Four other potters also stayed at the Pottery, three of them apparently living in the Pottery House with the Gardner family – John Wyllie (60), David Roy (50), and Robert Hardie (40); there was also a female servant. In the Pottery outhouse lived another potter Richard Ness (50), which he shared with James Stuart (30), who is simply listed as "Male Servant" and who may possibly have had some role as a pottery labourer. This first Census gave very limited information regarding places of birth, but it did indicate that John Gardner was a local man (and his four children were also local), whereas the other four potters living at Dunmore were not, nor were the three more living elsewhere. Nearby, at Dunmore Moss, was John Wyllie (45) – given the peculiar system of listing dates, he could have been nineteen years younger than his namesake, and therefore his son. He had a wife, two sons, and a daughter. Also at Dunmore Moss was James Brown (36), with his wife and three (or perhaps four) children. A little further distant, down on the Forth at Airth Shore, was William Boslem (30), with his wife and son. All eight of these pottery workers are simply given the designation "Potter"; the later Censuses were to be more specific as to the nature of their occupations.

1851 Census

Still at the head of affairs was John Gardner, aged 52, his occupation appearing as "Farmer of 27 acres employing 4 labourers, & Potter employing 9 men". Clearly, John Gardner leased a lot more land than that on which the Pottery stood, and he is listed as farmer first and potter second. This may be partially explained by the natural bias of the enumerator towards the former occupation, considering that by far the most common calling in the parish related to agriculture, but the proportion of Gardner's respective workers, 4 to 9, gives a more realistic indication of where his principal interest lay. He lived with his wife and three daughters, the eldest two of whom, aged 19 and 14, had left school, and are each listed as "Farmer & Potter's daughter". Peter is not mentioned. Three other potters lived at Dunmore Pottery: David Roy, "Potter (Thrower)", aged 62, unmarried, from Montrose; Andrew Gray, "Potter (Turner)", aged 45 from Dysart in Fife, with a wife and four daughters; and James Gormley, "Potter's Labourer", aged 21, unmarried, from Ireland. Completing the household were three agricultural labourers and a house servant. For reasons which will be given shortly, it is worth recording the names of the labourers. They were: James Moir, aged 45, a widower from Clackmannan; Charles Brown, aged 16, from Alloa; and Ebeneezer Ritchie, aged 12, from Perth. Other potters lived close by at Dunmore Moss, which supported two communities. At Dunmore Moss North, in Mackie's Houses, was Robert Merrilees, "Potter (Slip Pan Man)", aged 39 from Musselburgh, with a wife and daughter; and James Brown, "Potter (Finisher)", aged 46 from Ireland, with a wife, son, and three daughters. At Dunmore Moss South was James McKechnie, "Potter (Thrower)", aged 45 from Glasgow, with a wife and daughter. At Red Row, a small community a little further to the north, was Peter Gibson, "Potter (Finisher)", aged 34 from Inveresk in Midlothian, with a wife and two daughters. In Airth Village, was George A. Overend, "Labourer (Pottery)", aged 43 from England, with a wife, a son, and three daughters. It is worth noting that by this time, Dunmore Pottery was not the only ceramic industry operating in the parish, two Falkirk men having established a fire-clay pipe works.

1861 Census

Remaining in charge of the Pottery was John Gardner, now 62. Both his farm and his potworks had grown during the previous decade, for he is described as "Farmer of 50 acres employing 4 labourers and Potter Master employing 12 workers (9 men and 3 women)". Mrs Helen Gardner is listed as "Farmer & Potter's wife", and their daughters are similarly described. Again there is no mention of Peter. Also there were two unmarried men each called "Pottery Labourer" – James Gormley (aged 34 – thirteen years older since 1851!) from Ireland, and David Cook (18) from Falkirk. Finally, there were two female domestic servants and a ploughman. The house had six rooms with windows. Also at the Pottery, but in a separate unit (perhaps the outhouse), was another ploughman with his wife and family of four. It is worthy of note that the probable names of the four agricultural labourers are James Meikle, Robert Hardie, William Watson, and Charles McArthur, all of Dunmore. What is intriguing is that each was originally entered as a "Pottery Labourer" by the enumerator, only to have this changed to "Agric. Labourer", presumably by the registrar while checking the entries. However, Robert Hardie had been a pottery worker twenty years earlier. As the 1841 census did not specify classes of potter, he may have been a pottery labourer, but this does raise the suggestion that John Gardner, farmer and potter, may have had a flexible attitude towards the nature of work he gave to his unskilled employees, perhaps switching them around on a seasonal basis. Ten years later, James Meikle is listed as a fireman; twenty year later, Catherine McArthur is given as a fireman's widow. Thus it is possible that both these men were firemen (*i.e.* kilnmen) at the Pottery, though there is difficulty with that term, as we shall see shortly. Still at Dunmore Moss was James Brown, now 57, "Potter, Journeyman", with his wife, son, daughter, and grandson. Close by, at Moss-side, was Andrew Gray, who had moved out of the Pottery house. He is also given as "Potter, Journeyman". Ten years earlier, he and his wife had four daughters; by this time, they had five! The eldest, Mary A. Gray (17), is listed as "Pottery Worker". At South Moss was John Greig, "Potter (Journeyman)", aged 51 from Prestonpans, with his wife. Finally, at East End in Airth, there was James McLean, "Potter Thrower (Earthenware Journeyman)", aged 23 from Glasgow, with a wife and stepson. The Census also gives us two more potters' names, though neither was functioning at this time. At The Path in Airth, Susan McMahon, a 50 year old widow, lived with her unmarried daughter and her grandson; all three came from Ireland. She is described as "Pottery Labourer's widow". At South Moss was William Gardner, aged 75, a native of Airth parish, who lived with his wife Elizabeth, aged 70. He is listed as "Pauper (formerly Potter)". Considering his name, his trade, his birthplace, and his home, he surely must have been John Gardner's elder brother, formerly the proprietor of Alloa Pottery. One would therefore hope that his impecunious situation did not become too severe. (There is a sign that his circumstances did improve, for when he died in 1863, he was in Alloa.)

1871 Census

There was a change at the Pottery with the death of John Gardner in 1866. Peter had previously returned (where had he been for a dozen years or more?) to take over the running of the works; he is listed as "Master Potter employing 10 men & 3 boys". He evidently did not maintain the farming interests to the extent which his father had done (though other evidence points to a different conclusion), although the enumerator did not overlook this side of the work, giving the address of the works as "Dunmore Pottery and Farm House", and listing his mother Helen Gardner (69) as "formerly Farmer's and Potter's wife". Peter Gardner, now 34 (actually 37), remained unmarried. His elder sister, Margaret, had left home by this time, but the two younger ones remained – Helen (32) and Anne (28). They are each listed as "Farmer and Potter's daughter". This Census unfortunately slips back into the uninformative job descriptions of the first one in places, with "Potter" being the most commonly-used term. In addition to the master, the big house (now with seven windowed rooms) was home to three teenage pottery workers – James Hutton (19) from Falkirk, William Roberts (16) from Bathgate, and George Neilson (16) from Airdire. Completing the household was a domestic servant, a labourer (James Gormley, 45, from Ireland), and a carter (William Graham, 42, from Airth). If the farming side of the business really had been reduced, then these last two named men may be regarded as probable pottery workers. Living adjacent in Dunmore Pottery East Cottages were three more potters – William Wilson (22) from Stirling, with his wife, son, and two daughters; James McLean (34) from Glasgow, with his wife and five sons; and Thomas Campbell (32) from Glasgow, with his wife and five daughters. Also living there was the "Pottery Fireman" (*i.e.* kilnman), John Campbell (58) from Edinburgh, with his wife. Across the yard in the West Cottage lived two specialist pottery workers, with their adopted daughter – James Campbell (36) from Duddingston by Edinburgh, a "Presser & Mould Maker", and his wife Isabella (35) from Glasgow, a "Spout Maker in Pottery". This latter occupation indicates that teapots accounted for a major proportion of the Pottery's output. Isabella Campbell may well have made the handles as well, for the text of the booklet describes how teapots were produced in quantity by throwing the bodies and lids, and moulding the spouts, handles, and knobs, which were then added on by a specialist worker. In the Main Street of Airth lived James Gilfillan (34) from Muiravonside in Stirlingshire, a "Labourer at Pottery", with his wife and two daughters. Also in that street, living alone, was Margaret Brown (62), "formerly Pottery fireman's wife". Finally, it is noted that James Meikle, a pottery and/or agricultural labourer ten years earlier, is now listed as "Fireman or stoker" at Ferry Road new houses. If he had indeed worked at the Pottery, this gives an indication of the type of work he might have been doing. However, there are pitfalls here. A number of his neighbours in Ferry Road were railway workers, so there is the possibility of him having switched occupations. Moreover, one "fireman" listed in the next Census worked in the local coal mine and another in the merchant navy, while in the following one there is a "stoker of steam crane", so there are various options regarding the actual occupation to which these terms refer.

1881 Census

Peter Gardner, "Master Potter" (44), was head of affairs (his mother had died in 1878). His three sisters – Margaret (46), Helen (42), and Annie (39) lived with him. All unmarried, they are accorded no description. Two men with the title of "Potter's servant" (*i.e.* labourer) lived there also – David McFeet (24) from Stirling, and John Welsh (42) from Ireland. Two female domestic servants completed the household. Thus there were eight unmarried adults living in Dunmore Pottery House, which by now had eight windowed rooms. This Census does not specify the individual units of accommodation around the Pottery, but it indicates that there were eight in all in addition to the big house, though not all would have been detached. Here lived another nine pottery workers: William Harrison (52), "Pottery Turner" from England, with his wife, son and three daughters; John Wright (58), "Potter" from Ireland, with his wife; Thomas Harrison (25), "Potter" from England, with his wife and two children; Alexander Thomson (52), "Potter" from Prestonpans, with his wife; Thomas Campbell (43), "Potter" from Glasgow, with his wife, father-in-law (a pensioner), and four daughters, the eldest of whom, Jane (20), was a "Pottery Worker"; John Campbell (38), "Potter" from Glasgow, with his wife and two sons; Andrew McCowan (54), "Pottery Packer" from Comrie in Perthshire, a widower; and John Campbell (67), "Potter" from Portobello (which is close to Duddingston, which the previous Census had stated to be his birth-place), with his wife. Also living at the Pottery was a forester and his wife. Three other pottery workers lived elsewhere in Airth parish: at Red Row was James Gilfillan (42), "Potter" from Muiravonside, with his wife, son and daughter; and at The Pleasance was John McLay (67), "Labourer at Pottery" from Airth, a widower; and David Alexander (61), "Potter" from Kirkcaldy, also a widower. It is worth noting that there was a brickworks operating in the parish by this date. It is known that brickworks often produced items of simple domestic pottery, but considering the highly individual nature of Dunmore Pottery's production, it is very unlikely that there was any rivalry between the two concerns.

1891 Census

Peter Gardner remained in charge of the Pottery, aged 56, unmarried, and simply designated "Potter". For the first time (and quite exceptionally in the normal run of Census Returns) his precise place of birth is given – Dunmore Pottery. Only one sister remained with him: Ann (42), unmarried, is given the title "Housekeeper"; she had probably been fulfilling that role, in a shared capacity at least, for the previous quarter-century. Three unmarried potters also lived in the house, along with a female domestic servant. They were: Catherine McAdam (40), "Potter" of Stirling; William Whitehead (58), "Labourer" of Denny in Stirlingshire; and David McFeat (32 – name spelt differently from the last Census), "Carter" from Stirling. Despite the reduced number of people living in the Pottery House, it by now had nine windowed rooms, maintaining its growth of one such room per decade which it had sustained over the previous forty years. Curiously, the address was no longer Dunmore Pottery as it had been, but became the more topographical Moss Road. Another five pottery workers are listed as living in Moss Road, their accommodation presumably being the Pottery cottages as previously. They were: Alexander Thomson (62), "Potter" from Prestonpans, with his wife and two grandsons; Thomas Campbell (54), "Pottery Presser" from Glasgow, with his wife and four adult unmarried daughters, all of whom were employed; John Wright (60), "Potter" from Ireland, and his wife; Andrew

McCowan (67), "Pottery Packer" from Comrie, a widower; and William Harrison (62), "Potter" from England, with his wife and employed son. The only other potter in the parish lived quite close to the Pottery at Holly Walk: this was Thomas Harrison (35), "Potter" from England, with his wife, two sons, and three daughters. He had no doubt moved out of one of the Pottery cottages which he had previously occupied into a larger house to accommodate his growing family.

1901 Census

Peter Gardner, "Potter", was still there, and despite having 'aged' only eight years in the past decade (now given as 64, but actually 67), his failing health raises the question as to the extent of his active participation in the works by this time. The decline of the Pottery is underlined by the fact that no active potter remained in the Pottery House or any of the associated cottages. The only possible exception was Catherine McAdam (50), listed as "General Servant", who had been down as a "Potter" ten years before, and may have retained some measure of that involvement. The House had a notable visitor on the day of the Census – Robert Henderson (35), originally from Paisley, who was destined to take over Dunmore Pottery following the demise of Peter Gardner (see Figure 12). The three Pottery cottages were now occupied by a road surfaceman, a saw-miller, and a "Potter (Retired)" – John Wright (89) and his wife. (His age is highly suspect; he had only been down as 60 ten years earlier, when he should have been 68, and so in 1901 he should have been 78.) It is only when we get down to the Holly Walk Cottages that we find active potters: Thomas Harrison (45) was given as a "Potter (Presser & Finisher)"; his elder daughter, Jane F. Harrison (21) was a "Pottery Warehouse Girl"; and his younger daughter Sarah Harrison (17) was a "Potter's Assistant". His sons, unlike his daughters, did not follow him into the pottery-making business, though it is worth noting that they had secured local occupations: William (19) was a gardener, and Thomas L. Harrison (15) was "Stable boy at Mansion", which must surely refer to Dunmore Park. The youngest boy (8) was still at school.

Table of Dunmore Pottery workers, compiled from the Census Returns with a few additional names from the Valuation Rolls

(no claim is made as to completeness, either of names or dates)

Name of pottery worker (bold for those who may feature in the *Visit* booklet)	Class of pottery worker (the most descriptive term used) and relevant family members	Year of birth (sometimes approximate)	Place of birth (pottery towns in bold) (Airth signifies the parish rather than the town)	Year(s) name in Census
Alexander, David	Potter	1820	**Kirkcaldy**	1881
Boslem, William	Potter	1810		1841
Brown, Charles	?Pottery labourer	1835	**Alloa**	1851
Brown, James	Potter: finisher	1805	Ireland	1841
	first child	1833	**Portobello**	
	second child	1840	**Glasgow**	
Brown, ——	Kilnman	?1810	(deceased)	(1871)
Campbell, Isabella	Potter: spoutmaker	1836	**Glasgow**	1871
Campbell, James	Potter: presser and mould-maker	1835	Duddingston, Edinburgh (adjacent to **Portobello**)	1871
	wife	1836	**Glasgow**	
	child	1868	**Glasgow**	
Campbell, Jane	Pottery worker	1861	**Glasgow**	1881
Campbell, John	Kilnman	1813	**Portobello**	1871, 1881
Campbell, John	Potter	1843	**Glasgow**	1881
Campbell, Thomas	Potter: presser	1839	**Glasgow**	1871, 1891
Cook, David	Pottery labourer	1843	Falkirk	1861
Ford, William	Potter			V.R. 1893
Gardner, John	Master Potter	1798	Airth	1841, 1851, 1861
	wife	1801	**Musselburgh**	
Gardner, Peter	Master Potter	1837 (in fact, 1834)	Airth	1871, 1881, 1891, 1901
Gibson, Peter	Potter: finisher	1817	**Inveresk**, Midlothian	1851
Gilfillan, James	Pottery labourer/ potter	1837	Muiravonside, Stirlingshire	1871, 1881
Gormley, James	Pottery labourer	1830	Ireland	1851, 1861, 1871
Graham, William	Carter	1829	Airth	1871
Gray, Andrew	Potter: turner	1806	Dysart, Fife	1851, 1861
	first child	1844	**Alloa**	
	second child	1846	**Glasgow**	
Gray, Mary	Pottery worker	1844	**Alloa**	1861

Name	Occupation	Birth Year	Birthplace	Census Years
Greig, John	Potter: journeyman	1810	**Prestonpans**	1861
	wife	1801	**Glasgow**	
Hardie, Robert	Pottery labourer	1801	Edinburgh	1841, 1861
Harrison, Jane F.	Pottery warehouse girl	1880	**Glasgow**	1901
Harrison, Sarah	Potter's assistant	1884	Airth	1901
Harrison, Thomas	Potter	1856	England	1881, 1901
	wife	1858	**Glasgow**	
	first child	1878	**Glasgow**	
	second child	1880	**Glasgow**	
Harrison, William	Potter: turner	1829	England	1881, 1891
	four children	1868-1872	all **Alloa**	
Humphries, Levi	Kilnman			V.R. 1903
Hutton, David	Potter			V.R. 1896
Hutton, James	Potter	1852	Falkirk	1871
Meikle, James	?Pottery labourer	1830	Airth	1861
Merrilees, Robert	Potter:			
	slip pan operator	1812	**Musselburgh**	1851
	wife	1815	**Musselburgh**	
	child	1840	**Musselburgh**	
Moir, James	?Pottery labourer	1806	Clackmannan	1851
McAdam, Catherine	Potter	1851	Stirling	1891
McArthur, Charles	?Pottery labourer	1807	St Ninians, Stirlingshire	1861
McCowan, Andrew	Pottery packer	1827	Comrie, Perthshire	1881, 1891
McFeet, David	Pottery labourer/ carter	1857	Stirling	1881, 1891
McKechnie, James	Potter: thrower	1806	**Glasgow**	1851
McLay, John	Pottery labourer	1814	Airth	1881
McLean, Thomas	Potter: thrower	1838	**Glasgow**	1861, 1871
McMahon, ——	Pottery labourer	?1810	(deceased)	(1861)
Neilson, George	Potter	1855	Airdire	1871
Ness, Richard	Potter	1790		1841
Overend, George	Pottery labourer	1808	England	1851
Ritchie, Ebeneezer	?Pottery labourer	1839	Perth	1851
Roberts, William	Potter	1855	Bathgate	1871
Roy, David	Potter: thrower	1789	**Montrose**	1841, 1851
Smart, James	?Pottery labourer	1810		1841
Taylor, James	?Pottery labourer			V.R. 1886
Thomson, Alexander	Potter	1829	**Prestonpans**	1881, 1891
Watson, William	?Pottery labourer	1804	Airth	1861
Welsh, John	Pottery labourer	1839	Ireland	1881
Whitehead, William	?Pottery labourer	1833	Denny, Stirlingshire	1891
Wilson, William	Potter	1849	Stirling	1871
	first child	1867	**Alloa**	
	second child	1868	**Alloa**	
Wright, John	Potter	1823	Ireland	1881, 1891
Wyllie, John	Potter	1780		1841
Wyllie, John	Potter	1795		1841

Census Summary

Year	No. of named potters	No. living at the Pottery	No. living near the Pottery	No. living elsewhere in the parish	No. of dependents
1841	9	6	2	1	15
1851	9	4	4	1	24
1861	12	3	4	5	21
1871	11	10	0	1	24
1881	15	12	1	2	26
1891	10	9	1	0	13
1901	4	1	3	0	3

A cautionary note.

When searching the Valuation Rolls for mentions of John or Peter Gardner, potter, the eye can sometimes deceive the brain. The supposed surname can be excluded when the person referred to is Morris Fitzgerald, *gardener* to the Earl of Dunmore. Likewise, the supposed occupation must be treated in the same way when it applies to Lewis *Potter*, blacksmith in the stables at Airth Castle. Both of these coincidences occur in the Valuation Roll for the parish of Airth in 1879, when the hoped-for surname turned out to be an occupation, and vice versa.

Appendix B

Dunmore Pottery Kiln

The kiln of Dunmore Pottery (see Figure C33) has become almost totemic of the famous works, and would be even more so today if it still survived. It stood for more than half a century after its last firing, but its fate was sealed in 1974, as I reported in the magazine of the Scottish Pottery Society:

> 'Dunmore Pottery Kiln: RIP'
> The sad news is here recorded of the collapse of the kiln belonging to Peter Gardner's famous Dunmore Pottery, near Airth in Stirlingshire. This was due to 'natural causes'. Despite the efforts of the present owners of the property, a number of small trees which had grown up around the top of the kiln proved too entrenched to remove, and their powerful roots prised loose several large portions of brickwork. Thus weakened, the structure was unable to withstand the gale-force winds, and crashed to the ground. About a quarter of it is still standing (half the circumference, up to about half its original height), but this is so unstable that it is difficult to see how it could be preserved, and it
> is likely that nature will level this portion also before too long. A number of bricks from the collapsed section are marked BALD / ALLOA. It is indeed a pity that having avoided the demolition sledge-hammer which has destroyed so many of our old pottery buildings, this important edifice should meet the same fate as a result of neglect and decay. With the demise of the Dunmore Kiln, the twin bottle-kilns at Portobello now stand alone as monuments to the past age of Scottish pottery factories.[111]

In the following issue of the magazine, I reproduced four photographs which illustrated the semi-collapsed state of the kiln.[112] These were taken with black and white film on a very dull day, and are lacking in clarity, though one of them clearly shows the destructive power of the roots of a fairly mature silver birch (see Figure 57); its trunk had been sawn off, but too late to save the structure.

Figure 57

Figure 58

Figure 59

Figure 60

A few months earlier, the remains were also photographed by an industrial historian, Ken MacKay, and a selection of those prints, showing details of arched brickwork, are reproduced here (see Figures 58, 59, and 60). He had also visited Dunmore Pottery two years previously, in 1972, to photograph the tiled room (*vide supra*), and using shots of the (more or less) intact kiln which he took at that time, he was able to make reconstruction drawings, consisting of plan, elevation, and two sections (see Figures 61, 62, 63, and 64). These were published in an industrial heritage magazine, along with a brief note recording the kiln's demise: "Pottery Kiln, Dunmore. Tragically, this handsome kiln collapsed after a gale in January 1974".[113]

I was perhaps being a little unrealistic in the 'Dunmore Pottery Kiln: RIP' note in suggesting that natural forces would no doubt level the remains of the kiln. They surely would have done so in time, but not long afterwards the owner decided to bulldoze what was left, and build a caravan park on the site. The irony was that the succeeding owner, Bill Mitchell, not only had a keen interest in Dunmore Pottery but a knowledge of the building trade, and would have been happy to consolidate the surviving brickwork, but by that time there were no visible remains left. (I would also have to amend the concluding remark in that article about the demise of the Dunmore kiln leaving only two extant industrial pottery kilns in Scotland. The older of the pair at Portobello had its top half taken down due to a misreading of its condition; the bricks were then stored insecurely resulting in many being broken and/or dispersed, so that eventually it had to be rebuilt, rather poorly, using new bricks. This means that only one and a half kilns remain as testimony to Scotland's erstwhile pottery industry.)

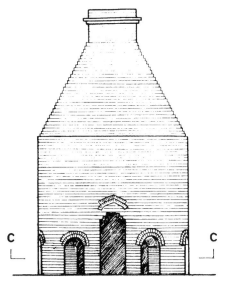

Figure 62

B ⌐

A ⌐   ⌐ A

B ⌐

Figure 61

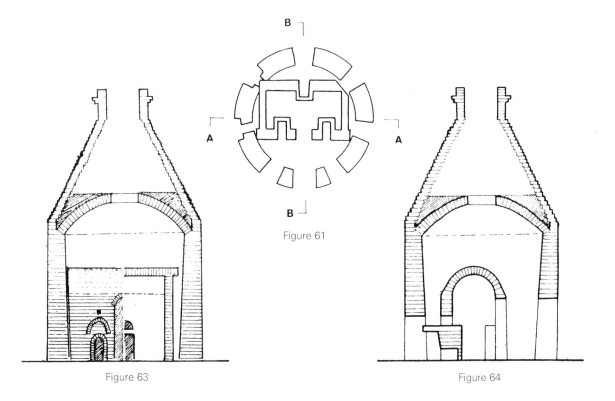

Figure 63

Figure 64

0   10   20
Scale in feet

111

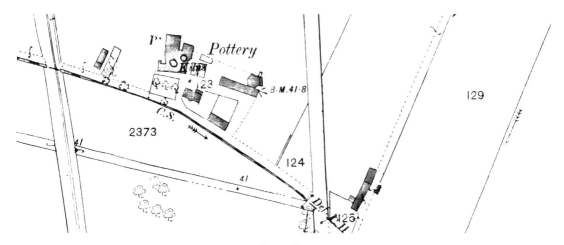

Figure 65

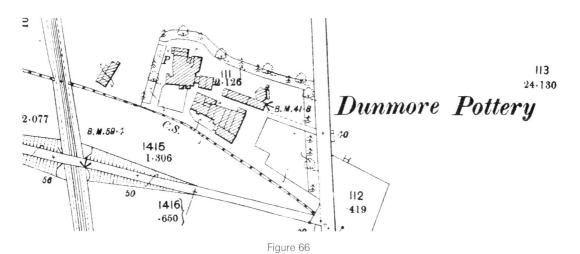

Dunmore Pottery

Figure 66

Dunmore Pottery

Figure 67

Such has been the interest in the Dunmore Pottery kiln, that usually overlooked is the fact that it did not stand alone: there were two. This is very evident from Ordnance Survey maps. The first edition 25-inch map, surveyed in 1859/60, clearly shows two kilns (see Figure 65). Interestingly, they are not of equal size; they also appear to have been rather poorly drawn (by the high standards of the Ordnance Survey), and are by no means perfectly circular, but confirmation of what they are is given by the caption, which reads "Kilns". The layout of the pottery dates from before the period of Peter Gardner, and it is no surprise to find that by the end of the century, the complex of buildings had become considerably enlarged, as shown on the second edition map, which was surveyed in 1895 (see Figure 66). The approach to the works had been changed; previously coming from the south-east, it was now more from an easterly direction. Despite the detail shown on the map, no kilns were delineated this time. They were both still there, however, and appear on the next edition, which was surveyed in 1913 (see Figure 67). They are properly circular this time, in precisely the same positions as previously, and still of distinctly different sizes. No kilns are shown on the 1960 edition, though the building which housed them is still there. Not surprisingly, the complex had shrunk somewhat, and ominously the word "Ruin" appears three times; the surprise is that the place is still captioned "Dunmore Pottery" fully forty years after production ceased, without the addition of "disused" or "site of " as was normal practice by the Ordnance Survey under such circumstances. There is the possibility that we have visual confirmation of the second kiln. In the old photograph of Dunmore Pottery House (see Figure 28), between the main kiln and the large tree to the left of the House, a shape appears over the top of a bush in the garden which resembles the top of the main kiln – a dark horizontal line, which is presumably a shadow caused by the protruding ring of brickwork just below the rim. The O.S. maps show the second kiln to have had a narrower diameter, which presumably meant that it was of lesser height, and also to have been further away from the viewpoint of the photograph, all of which means that it would have appeared considerably shorter. If the dark line does indeed represent the top of the second kiln, it appears in just the right location.

The existence of a second kiln gives a degree of superficial credibility to stories of Peter Gardner having exclusive access to a secondary smaller kiln, in which he would try out novel techniques, or fire items carrying experimental glazes to which only he had the recipe, and only he was able to view the results initially. So strong did this story become that when the *Falkirk Herald* produced an article on Dunmore Pottery in 1980, it appeared under the large headline 'Pottery's secret lost with death of Peter Gardner', and it is not hard to guess what the secret involved: "As the years went past, age began to take its toll of Peter Gardner until he was eventually forced to retire and, alas, the secret of the glaze was lost forever when he died".[114] (As with so many other writers, the surname was misspelt; it is here corrected.) Contemporary confirmation of this is given by James Paton in an article published in 1888, in which he speaks of "the brilliant colours of the glazes of which Mr Gardner possesses the secret".[115] In such circumstances, the question arises: does the story explain the reason for the second, smaller kiln, or has it been created in order to account for it? It is another version of the old chicken-and-egg conundrum. Being interested as to the source of the information, I quizzed the reporter, John Jenkinson, who told me that it came from his mother and her sisters, who had been raised in Larbert and

Stenhousemuir. She had lived into her nineties and they had both been centenarians, and they could all remember Dunmore Pottery in operation in the days of their youth. Stories of Peter Gardner and his secret recipes and firings were apparently well known throughout the district. Oral history, in the form of recollections, is more highly regarded nowadays that it was formally, and while it can hardly be taken as providing proof, it does at least offer a modicum of confirmation.

There has even been talk of yet another kiln at Dunmore. Writing in *The Lady* magazine in 1967, Oonagh Morrison describes how she was drawn to the site of the Pottery by "a strange cylindrical brick structure, rather like an elongated beehive, cracked, crumbling, and overgrown with moss and weeds. It had three apertures at the base and seemed to be open at the top. Must be a kiln, I thought. [Correct]…I drove up to have a closer look at the sadly dilapidated relic. An old man was pottering about the yard. He confirmed my surmise that this was the old pottery, and he told me that the kiln was one of three which had stood here at one time".[116] The lack of corroboration means that this statement should be regarded with a degree of scepticism.

Returning to the narrative of the *Visit* booklet, the reporter was less than accurate in the description of the kiln: "a circular building with a domed roof". Circular certainly, but the 'roof' was the typical Scottish cone, sitting on top of a cylinder, with the apex cut away to accommodate the stubby chimney. The impression of a domed roof was obviously gained by viewing the structure from the inside, but it was the 'ceiling' which would have provided the domed effect, as can be seen in the reconstruction drawings of the kiln when shown in section (see Figures 63 and 64). This shallow dome effect is sometimes known as a saucer dome. That the reporter was not shown the second kiln lends support to the story regarding secret firings of experimental glazes. If anything still remains underground of this mysterious kiln, excavation could well reveal material evidence to confirm the legend. Regarding the main kiln, it would be appropriate if its foundations were uncovered and preserved as an on-site memorial to the remarkable products which emanated from it, and to the equally remarkable man whose genius created them.

Appendix C

Dunmore Ware at the Edinburgh International Exhibition of 1886

No concept is more redolent of the Victorian era than that of the major industrial exhibition. The classic prototype and supreme catalyst was the Great Exhibition held at the Crystal Palace in London in 1851, which sparked off a world-wide enthusiasm for such events. Scotland was not to be outdone, and after a couple of specialist international exhibitions had been staged in Edinburgh in the early 1880s, it was decided to organise a major industrial exhibition in the Capital. A subscription fund quickly exceeded its target, and soon a huge structure occupied the western half of The Meadows (an area of flat grassland half a mile south of Edinburgh Castle, occupying the site of the former Burgh Loch). The Edinburgh International Exhibition of Industry, Science, and Art ran from 6th May to 30th October 1886, and proved to be a huge commercial and popular success, receiving more than two and three-quarter million visitors.

The exhibition was fronted by a palatial edifice known as the Grand Hall, with rows of bays stretching out behind it (see Figure 68). The exhibits were divided into sixteen classes, Class II being Pottery, Glass, and Kindred Industries; within that, Section 2 dealt with earthenware and stoneware. The Official Catalogue of the Exhibition lists all the exhibitors (2,229 in total),

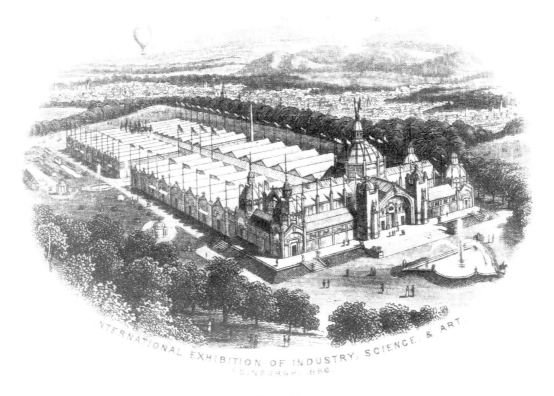

Figure 68

with a brief description of what they had on display. The entry for stall No. 83 (the first exhibit in the Central Court) reads as follows:

> "**Gardner, Peter**, Dunmore Pottery, *via* Stirling. – Pottery consisting of Vases, Baskets, Brackets, Pots, Teapots, Tea Sets, Candlesticks, Medallions, Cheese Dishes, Bread and Fruit Plates, Garden Seats, Umbrella Stands, Pedestals, etc." (p.47).

The Official Guide to the Exhibition describes the displays in greater or lesser detail; in the case of Dunmore Pottery, it is complimentary though disappointingly brief: "The Dunmore Pottery Stall displays some attractive novelties" (p.30).

The exhibition, in addition to displaying and acting as a point of sale for the products of the exhibitors, was given a competitive edge by the introduction of an award system, with prizes being bestowed on those firms which gained special praise from panels of jurors. Peter Gardner was no doubt gratified to find that his efforts were appreciated, and he was awarded a Silver Medal diploma, which was the third-highest category (for a drawing of the medal, see Figure 69). In the Official List of Jurors' Awards, some entries give details of particular items which caught the eye of the judges, but the one for Dunmore pottery could not be briefer, merely

Figure 69

reading "Pottery" – and they also managed to misspell his name (p.17). The *Scotsman* reporter was likewise rather taken with these wares, though commenting only in general terms: "From the Dunmore Pottery many splendid specimens of vases and other artistic work are shown, all in the shape of articles of general utility and beautiful finish".[117]

Dunmore pottery made a further appearance in the Exhibition, in a special section called 'Old Edinburgh'. This consisted of a street composed of reconstructions of famous buildings which had once featured in the history of the city, but which had been demolished. The street was designed by the noted Edinburgh architect Sydney Mitchell (1856-1930), who had only set up on his own three years earlier. He took every care to ensure that the reconstructed buildings were faithful representations of those which had once existed. It was intended by the Exhibition organisers that this would not merely be a sterile exhibit, but that it should also act as a display location. Exhibitors here were required to harmonise their efforts with the atmosphere created by the street; they had to indicate clearly the corporation, guild, or craft which was being represented, and those attending the stalls had to be attired in costume appropriate to their period and craft. Among those listed in the Official Guide to the Exhibition as occupying premises in 'Old Edinburgh' is, at No. 6:

> "**Gardiner** [*sic*], **Peter**, Dunmore Pottery Co., Princes Street, Edinburgh. – Dunmore Pottery" (p.293).

It is odd that the address (presumably of his depot) is given as Princes Street, and may well represent a stop-gap venue between his periods of tenure in Castle Street and George Street, when there is a void in the Post Office Directories regarding his bases in Edinburgh (as noted when dealing with the Frontispiece, section III).

While most of the reconstructed buildings in 'Old Edinburgh' were of some historical fame or notoriety, the ground plan of the street merely refers to No. 6, the premises occupied by Peter Gardner, by the uninformative title of "Nameless House from Cowgate". The *Book of Old Edinburgh* does not provide much more, simply noting that "There is no historical clue all down the centuries to any inhabitant of this house," though it does offer a modicum of praise for the building itself: "It is a good specimen of picturesque street architecture attained by simple means".[118] We can actually see what it looks like, thanks to a photograph by Marshall Wane.

Figure 70

Figure 71

For some reason, the authorities banned photography in the Exhibition proper, but Wane secured a monopoly to publish photographs taken in 'Old Edinburgh', and thus we get an impression of the architectural character of the premises which Peter Gardner occupied there (see Figure 70). It had the attractive feature of a bowed-out display window, one of several in the street. The pity is that, even with the advantage of considerable magnification (see Figure 71), no items of Dunmore pottery may be discerned inside.

It must have been a fairly late decision to have Dunmore products in this section of the exhibition as well as in the Central Court, because the lease for No. 6 in 'Old Edinburgh' is not in favour of Peter Gardner but of Jessie Robertson of 20 Earl Grey Street, Edinburgh, which was the address for Baird, Matthew & Co., auctioneers and valuators. The lease document specifies that it was rented for the purpose of "Exhibiting and selling pottery of all kinds".[119] However, she did not take up the lease, though she did feature in the main Exhibition, where she was to be found at stall No. 104 in the Central Court. There she displayed fancy china, peacocks and swans being a speciality. Thus the character of the goods on show in No. 6 'Old Edinburgh' was not greatly altered, considering the exotic shapes produced at Dunmore, though whether this was achieved by planning or was merely fortuitous is not known. Nor do we know why Jessie Robertson pulled out of 'Old Edinburgh' before the opening; perhaps she found the special rentals for this section too high, and certainly the £51 6s. charged for No. 6 was a considerable sum. It did not deter Peter Gardner, however, and he surely must have benefited from exhibiting in such a prestigious location, though presumably only in a retail capacity; unlike several other trades represented in the Exhibition, there is no suggestion that pottery was actually made here.

An interesting sideline to the main activities of the Exhibition was the publication of a number of satirical booklets. These consist mainly of cartoon sketches, accompanied by captions which display a love of dreadful puns, a pawky sense of humour, and a distinct send-up of what the artists seemingly considered the pompous attitude of some of the exhibitors and senior members of the organising committee. Typical of this type of production is a booklet of lithographs entitled *Sketches at the International Exhibition, Edinburgh, 1886*, drawn by W. Stevenson, ARSA, and published by Marshall Wane at his premises at 82 George Street, Edinburgh. This booklet differs from similar efforts by having a straightforward cover, but inside it is every bit as satirical, the pencil sketches (which are of a reasonable standard) having captions which seem to have drawn the worst in awful puns out of the artist – but they are quite fun, nevertheless. William Grant Stevenson (1849-1919) came from Ratho in West Lothian, and trained at the Royal Scottish Academy Schools in Edinburgh, becoming a noted sculptor and artist. His studio was at 13 Dalry Road, Edinburgh. His oil paintings often display a humorous touch, and this trait is very evident in the illustrations which he drew for this booklet. Fortunately, he stopped to sketch at one of the pottery stands, and identified it by including its sign, which proclaimed "DUNMORE POTTERY", though sadly he did not make a legible copy of the two subsidiary lines of writing. Quite a few items of pottery may be discerned, including bowls and vases, and prominently featured is a large pot on a pedestal (see Figure 72).

Figure 72   SOMETHING SCOTCH

Figure 73

It might be thought that Dunmore products are so striking that once on display, they were quite capable of speaking for themselves, but Peter Gardner, who clearly had a keen awareness of the value of publicity, liked to drive home the point. In his first exhibition, held at the Highland Show of 1874 in Inverness, a reporter was impressed by the sales technique which he employed: "the young lady who superintended the sale did all in her power to make the goods attractive".[120] Stevenson's sketch at the 1886 Exhibition shows such a lady sales assistant; she is clad in a feathered Glengarry, a jacket with tartan plaid held in place by a large shoulder-brooch, and a full-length tartan skirt. All this amounted to a show of nationalism which the artist apparently deemed to be jingoistic – hence the somewhat scornful caption: "Something Scotch". The tartan worn may well have been appropriate to the task if Peter Gardner adopted the same policy as he did two years later at the Glasgow International Exhibition: "The stand is in charge of a young lady, in Highland dress of Murray tartan, Murray being the family name of Lord Dunmore, on whose property the pottery is situated".[121] It is interesting to contrast Stevenson's sketch with a rather similar one made a few months later in connection with the Dunmore display at the Glasgow Industrial Exhibition of 1886 which was held at Burnbank. A satirical Glasgow journal called *Quiz* featured a page of humorous sketches relating to this exhibition, with the general title of "The Busy Bees of Burnbank". The signature of the cartoonist reads 'Twym', which was the pseudonym of Alexander Stuart Boyd (1854-1930), a Glasgow artist and illustrator. In very sketchy form, we see a display of pottery under the heading "DUNMORE", attended to by a lady clad in a similar outfit to that of her Edinburgh counterpart, though the Glasgow figure is very different in attitude. The former sketch is very staid, apart perhaps from its tongue-in-cheek caption, while the latter has a more mystical quality. The Dunmore ladies are dressed in near identical costume, but while the Edinburgh matron has her feet planted firmly on the ground, the Glasgow damsel floats aloft, representing 'The Spirit of Pottery', as the whimsical caption would have it (see Figure 73).

Dunmore pottery received special attention on 26th May 1886, when the Edinburgh International Exhibition was visited by the Lord High Commissioner to the General Assembly of the Church of Scotland. His wife, Lady Thurlow, had her ancestral seat at Kinnaird, a little over two miles south of Dunmore Pottery. The organisers felt that local industries would be of special interest to the distinguished couple, and so they were given the opportunity to examine stalls displaying Carron ironwork and Dunmore pottery. The *Scotsman* reporter noted: "The party also stopped to examine and admire the exhibit from the Dunmore Pottery, in the neighbourhood of Kinnaird, and Mr Peter Gardiner [*sic*], the proprietor, had the honour of being introduced to Lord and Lady Thurlow".[122]

The biggest moment for the Exhibition in general, and for Peter Gardner in particular, came on 18th /19th August, when it was visited by its patron, Queen Victoria. At one time, it had been hoped that she would perform the official opening on 6th May, but as she was due to perform similar tasks at the Colonial and Indian Exhibition in London two days beforehand, and at the International Exhibition of Navigation, Commerce, and Industry in Liverpool five days later, the ceremonial responsibility was given to her grandson, Prince Albert Victor. It was therefore a matter of great pleasure when the Chairman of the Exhibition's Executive Council was informed by letter on 1st May that the Queen intended to visit the Edinburgh Exhibition in the course of her autumn journey to Balmoral. When the day came, the city was decorated in festive fashion, huge crowds lined the route from the Palace of Holyroodhouse to The Meadows, and a vast throng of about 20,000 people assembled in the Exhibition grounds to greet her as she arrived to tour the Exhibition.

It may be remembered that the booklet *A Visit to Dunmore Pottery* made a forthright claim regarding that occasion: "When the Queen visited the Edinburgh Exhibition she made extensive purchases of Dunmore ware, the turquoise blue and the light red and the new crackled ware being specially chosen by her. The vase called the 'Queen's Vase' was a shape she admired, and also the grotesque-looking stand for ferns called the 'Dunmore Toad' ". However, despite very detailed accounts of both the Queen's official visit and private visit appearing in *The Scotsman*, there is no mention of her showing any interest in Dunmore Pottery. Considering the close attention paid to her every move and the extensive nature of the reporting, it would seem that the claim made in the *Visit* booklet lacks supporting evidence. Fortuitously, confirmation is provided in a tiny paragraph contained in a section of *Scotsman* miscellaneous notes which appeared on the day after the Queen's private visit: "Mr Gardner of Dunmore Pottery received orders through Dean of Guild Gowans [James Gowans, Chairman of the Executive Council of the Exhibition Association] to proceed to Holyrood with specimens of his goods for Her Majesty to select from".[123]

Clearly, the Queen had at least shot an admiring glance at the Dunmore display, though it was apparently undetected by the eagle-eyed Press corps. Disappointingly, the Surveyor of the Queen's Works of Art can find no trace at present of any items of Dunmore ware anywhere in the Royal Collections, even though specific colours and named shapes are detailed in the booklet. A spokesperson at St James's Palace, home of the Royal Collection Trust, reckons that the most likely explanation for the absence of these pieces is that they were bought by the Queen not for herself, but for use as presents.[124]   Nevertheless, we now know that the statement made in the booklet's Proclamation about Dunmore having secured "the distinguished patronage of Her Most Gracious Majesty the Queen" was no idle boast, and this must have secured Peter Gardner's future as a potter whose renown would be unsurpassed.

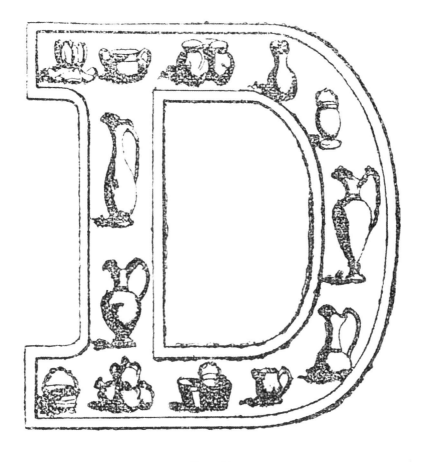

Figure 74

References

1 An example would be Arthur Coysh, *British Art Pottery, 1870-1940* (Newton Abbott, 1976), pp.50-51; very brief, and littered with inaccuracies repeated from earlier deficient accounts.

2 *[Old] Statistical Account of Scotland*, Parish of Airth, vol. III, pp.487 and 488.

3 Fieldwork conducted by Professor David Smith of Coventry University in the 1990s.

4 see William Nimmo, *History of Stirlingshire*, 3rd edn., ed. Richard Gillespie (Glasgow, 1880), vol. I, p.336.

5 *Third Statistical Account of Scotland*, Parish of Airth, vol. XVIII, p.410.

6 Sir Robert Sibbald, *History and Description of Stirlingshire*, p.48, being Book II of his *History of the Sheriffdoms of Linlithgow and Stirling* (Edinburgh, 1710; the date 1707 given in the 1892 reprint is incorrect).

7 see Graeme Cruickshank, 'Throsk Brick and Tile Works: some details of late 19th century production' (forthcoming).

8 see David Caldwell and Valerie Dean, 'The pottery industry at Throsk, Stirlingshire, in the 17th and early 18th century' in *Post-Medieval Archaeology* No. 26, 1992, pp.1-46.

9 see Arthur Mitchell (ed.), *Geographical Collections relating to Scotland, made by Walter MacFarlane* (Edinburgh, 1906), vol. I, pp.328 and 329. See also Thomas Miller, 'The Diary of Alexander Johnstone of Kirkland, 1723-26' in *Records of the Scottish Church History Society* vol. IV, 1932, pp.267-72, but there is no mention of the potters of Elphingstone.

10 William Nimmo, *General History of Stirlingshire* (Edinburgh, 1777), p.460.

11 *New Statistical Account of Scotland*, Parish of Airth, vol. VIII, p.285.

12 *Third Statistical Account of Scotland*, Parish of Airth, vol. XVIII, p.411.

13 Archibald McMichael, *Past and Present: a descriptive and historical account of Stirling, Dumbarton, and Linlithgowshires* (Glasgow, n.d. [1888 x 91], p.53.

14 for the Gardner family tree, see James Spreull and Robert Rankine, *Alloa Pottery* (Clackmannan District Libraries, Alloa, 1993), p.8. This is useful regarding the history of both Alloa Pottery and Dunmore Pottery.

15 Old Parish Register, County of Stirling, Parish of Airth (469/5), *f*.13 (General Register Office for Scotland, Edinburgh).

16 Arnold Fleming, *Scottish Pottery* (Glasgow, 1923), p.200.

17 *Art Journal*, new series, vol. XIX, 1880, p.156.

18 in the year 1797, according to Falkirk Museums, cited in the text of an exhibition poster (1988), and in *Local Ceramics...in the Falkirk District* by Geoff Bailey (2002), p.7. Exact reference not known (it is not in the Old Parish Register recording the birth of John Gardner in 1797, nor in the Kirk Session Book for that year). See also ref. no. 14.

19 Particular Register of Sasines for the Shire of Stirling, vol. 324, *f*.212 (H.M. General Register House, Edinburgh).

20 *[Old] Statistical Account of Scotland*, Parish of Kelton, vol. III, p.305n.

21   Registered Design No. 305150 (Series A), 9th November 1876.

22   *Alloa Journal*, 8th July 1876. (The Exhibition opened on 10th May.)

23   *ibid.* ref. no. 17.

24   Geoffrey Godden (ed.), *Jewitt's Ceramic Art of Great Britain* (London, 1972), p.147.

25   *Pottery Gazette*, 1st October 1883, p.956

26   *Pottery Gazette Diary*, 1882, p.31.

27   E. Lloyd Thomas, *Victorian Art Pottery* (London, 1974), p.3.
28   *op.cit.*, pp.149-50.
29   do., p.14.
30   do., p.7, quoting "a lecture published in 1883", but no further source given. This lecture has not been traced in the following works: Temple Scott, *A Bibliography of the Works of William Morris* (London, 1897); Aymer Vallance, *William Morris: his art, his writings, and his public life* (London, 1897), Appendix I: 'Chronological List of the Printed Works of William Morris'. Sometimes unpublished lectures received lengthy reviews, but no promising title is contained in Eugene LeMire, *The Unpublished Lectures of William Morris* (Detroit, 1969), Appendix I, 'A Calendar of William Morris's Platform Career', *sub anno* 1883 (though the list is far from complete). Likewise, there is no likely entry in Nicholas Salmon, *The William Morris Chronology* (Bristol, 1996) for that year, though on 23rd July he did visit an exhibition of pottery and sculpture by George Tinworth of the Doulton Pottery at Lambeth in London, one of whose specialities was modelling figurines of animals engaged in human pastimes (cf. the singing frog of Dunmore, see Figure C1). The general sentiments alluded to by Morris in Lloyd Thomas's interpretation of his five canons of craft-made pottery were expressed in a lecture entitled 'Art, Wealth, and Riches', which was delivered on 6th March 1883 and published later that year in the *Manchester Quarterly: a journal of literature and art* (vol. II, pp.153-75). According to the *Morris Chronology* (*vide supra*), this was the only one of his lectures to be published in 1883. Likewise, the lecture referred to by Thomas is not known to the William Morris Society. This important issue therefore remains unresolved at the present time.

31   cited in Brian Watters, 'Dunmore Pottery' in *Calatria* (Journal of the Falkirk Local History Society) No. 15, Autumn 2001, p.105.

32   *Falkirk Herald*, 12th May 1888.

33   James Paton, *Glasgow Herald*, 26th July 1888.

34   National Library of Scotland MS.7429. This letter is reproduced *op.cit.* ref. no. 14, p.14.

35   My thanks to Fiona Hayes of the People's Palace Museum for this information.

36   for an illustration and discussion of this piece, see Simon Olding and Zoë Capernaros, 'A Remarkable Dunmore Plaque' in *Scottish Pottery Historical Review* No. 7, 1982, pp.9-11.

37   Barbara Davidson, technical notes, Dunmore Pottery Exhibition, Stirling Smith Art Gallery & Museum, Summer/Autumn 2002.

38   *op.cit.* ref. no. 16, p.202.

39   Sasine Abstract, dated 2nd May 1879, No. 3674.
40   *loc.cit.*, 29th November 1884, No.3332.
41   do., 30th May 1889, No.3303.
42   do., 1st March 1899, No. 157.
43   do., 20th May 1890, No. 4296; 6th November 1897, No. 1088.

Note: the Register of Sasines, a series of bound volumes of manuscript collations, merely expands the printed abstracts with a plethora of legal jargon, and although they give a more exact description of the boundaries of the properties referred to, they seldom add anything of historical significance to the basic summary given in the Abstracts. (H.M. General Register House, Edinburgh.)

44   *Falkirk Herald*, 30th August 1902.

45   *op.cit*. ref. no. 16, pp.202 and 203.

46   Charles Lamburn (publ.), *Stirlingshire, Dumbartonshire, and Linlithgowshire Business Directory for 1893-94* (Edinburgh, ?1893), p.4.

47   Graeme Cruickshank, 'On the importance of being marked…' in *Scottish Pottery Society Archive News* No. 2, 1977, p.13.

48   for a description of this saut bucket and an illustration of the complete maker's mark, see Graeme Cruickshank, 'Marked Redware' in *Scottish Pottery Historical Review* No. 5, 1980, p.39; for a sketch of the decorative feature depicting a sail/steam-ship, see Robin Hill, *On Dunmore Pottery* (Kippen, 1979), [p.1].

49   see Vicary Gibbs (ed.), *The Complete Peerage* (London, 1916), vol. IV, pp.545-6.

50   Dunmore Muniments (privately held), Section I, Box IV, item 59.

51   Sir Sidney Lee, *King Edward VII: a biography* (London, 1925), vol. II, pp.394-5.

52   *op.cit*. ref. no.16, p.201.

53   for example, see *op.cit*. ref. no. 31, p.109, n.11. My thanks to Brian Watters for directing me to the precise sources: for the earliest known record of the Prince of Wales at Dunmore Park, see *Falkirk Herald & Linlithgow Journal*, 20th October 1870; for preparations for the visit three years later, see *op.cit*., 24th April 1873, and for its cancellation, see *op.cit*., 3rd July 1873.

54   *Stirling Journal & Advertiser*, 15th September 1876.

55   *op.cit*. ref. no. 51, vol. II, pp.416 and 424.

56   *op.cit*. ref. no. 16, p.202.

57   MS. Prince of Wales' Diary, *sub anno* 1876. (The Royal Archives, Windsor Castle.)

58   *op.cit*. ref. no. 16, p.201.

59   John Jenkinson, 'Pottery's secret lost with the death of Peter Gardiner [*sic*]' in the *Falkirk Herald*, 19th September 1980.

60   *op.cit*. ref. no. 16, p.201.
61   do., p.202.

62   see Robin Hill, *On Dunmore Pottery* (Kippen, 1979), [p.2].

63   Geoffrey Hay and Geoffrey Stell, *Monuments of Industry* (RCAHMS, Edinburgh, 1986), p.173.
64   see *op.cit*., p.174.

65   RCAHMS photo ST/2723.

66   Oonagh Morrison, 'Dunmore – An Old Pottery in the Carse of Stirling' in *Scotland's Magazine*, August 1966, p.43.

67   RCAHMS record sheets, Stirlingshire, Dunmore Pottery.

68   Oonagh Morrison, 'Potter's Cottage' [her odd description of Dunmore Pottery House] in *The Lady*, 23rd November 1967, p.813.

69   Huntly House Museum, Edinburgh, acc. nos. 4023-6/79.

70   *Falkirk Herald*, 12th May 1888.

71   *op.cit.* ref. no. 16, pp.201 and 202.

72   pers. comm. from Anne Countess of Dunmore.

73   *ibid.* ref. no. 17.

74   see *Stirling Observer*, 3rd August 1854.
75   see *loc.cit.*, 31st May 1855.
76   *loc.cit.*, 27th November 1856.

77   as ref. no. 72.

78   *Stirling Journal & Advertiser*, 26th February 1886.

79   Peter Davis and Robert Rankine, *Wemyss Ware* (Edinburgh, 1986), pp.9 and 102.

80   National Archives of Scotland, RHP 4409/1 (catalogue) and 2 (map).

81   General Register of Sasines, 22nd January 1875 (copy extract in the Dunmore Muniments).

82   *The Times*, 28th August 1907.

83   dates given in R. Butt, *Directory of Railway Stations* (Sparkford, 1995), pp.14 and 54.

84   This note has been put together using various sources, principally Peter Marshall, *The Scottish Central Railway* (Usk, 1998) and Gordon Stansfield, *Stirlingshire and Clackmannanshire's Lost Railways* (Catrine, 2002). For maps, see Clifford Wignall, *Complete British Railways Maps and Gazetteer, 1830-1981* (Oxford, 1983), pp.46 and 50.

85   *Pottery Gazette Diary*, 1882, p.31.

86   This note is largely based on an article by Lewis Lawson in the *Falkirk Herald*, 7th September 1968.

87   Sinclair Dunn, *The Auld Scotch Songs and Ballads* (Glasgow, 1895), p.56.

88   *op.cit.* ref. no. 4, p.333.

89   *op.cit.* ref. no. 16, p.201.
90   do., p.200.
91   do., p.201.

92   see Graeme Cruickshank, 'Revealing Dunmore Debris: on-site information concerning Dunmore pottery production' in *Calatria* (Journal of the Falkirk Local History Society), forthcoming (probably No. 17, Autumn 2002).

93   *op.cit.* ref. no. 16, p.57.

94   My thanks to Robert Rankine for this suggestion.
95   The Bible, Book of Isaiah, chapter 4, verse 25.
96   do., Book of Chronicles, volume I, chapter 4, verse 23.
97   do., Book of Jeremiah, chapter 18, verses 1-6.

98   summarised from Rostislav Holthoer, *New Kingdom Pharonic Sites. The Pottery* (Scandinavian Joint Expedition to Sudanese Nubia) vol. V, pt. 1 ([Stockholm] 1977), pp.7-8.

99   see Georg Steindorff, *Das Grab des Ti* (Leipzig, 1913), Plate 84.

100   *Colonial and Indian Exhibition, 1886; Empire of India Special Catalogue of Exhibits* (London, 1886), pp.316-7.

101   *Art Journal*, new series, 1886, p.191.

102   James Paton, *Glasgow Herald*, 31st May 1888.

103   for an illustration, see E. Lloyd Thomas, *Victorian Art Pottery* (London, 1974), Figure 17, p.180. The plaque itself was preserved in Southall Library, but that building is currently undergoing a major refurbishment; the plaque is in store at the time of writing, and its future display location has yet to be decided.

104   see Robert Shearer (publ.), *Officiale Hand Boke of Ye Strivelin Fancye Fayre* (Stirling, 1882), p.xxxix.

105   Peter Denholm, 'Firing a Bottle Oven' in *Scottish Pottery Society Archive News* No. 4, 1979, p.68.

106   *op.cit*. ref. no. 16, pp.200 and 201.
107   do., p.201.
108   do., p.201-2

109   see *Burmantofts Pottery* (Bradford and Leeds Museums, *ca.* 1983), catalogue no. 29, and illustrated on the cover (front centre).

110   see Julian Halsby and Paul Harris, *Dictionary of Scottish Painters, 1600 to the present* (Edinburgh, 1990), p.204; also Julian Halsby, *Scottish Watercolours, 1740-1940* (London, 1986), p.283. My thanks also to Michael McGinnes of Stirling Museum for providing additional information.

111   *Scottish Pottery Society Archivist's Newsletter* No. 1, 1976, pp.8-9.

112   *Scottish Pottery Society Archive News* No. 2, 1977, plate page between pp.11 and 12.

113   *Newsletter of the Scottish Society for Industrial Archaeology and the Scottish Society for the Preservation of Historical Machinery* (since amalgamated to become the Scottish Industrial Heritage Society) No. 6, pt. 1, July 1974, text p.17, illustrations p.18.

114   *ibid*. ref. no. 59.

115   *ibid*. ref. no. 33

116   *ibid*. ref. no. 68.

117   *The Scotsman*, 25th May 1886.

118   John and Alison Dunlop, *The Book of Old Edinburgh* (Edinburgh, 1886), pp.41-2.

119   Edinburgh City Archives, acc. no. 423.

120   *Stirling Journal & Advertiser*, 4th August 1874.

121   *Falkirk Herald*, 12th May 1888.

122   *The Scotsman*, 27th May 1886.

123   *The Scotsman*, 20th August 1886; see also *Falkirk Herald*, 12th May 1888.

124   pers. comm. from Henrietta Hudson, Assistant to the Deputy Surveyor of the Queen's Works of Art.